POTLUCK COOKERY

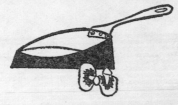

320 answers to the problems of "leftovers"—
answers to "nothing-in-the-house" puzzle—
money-saving—
time-saving—
easy-to-follow—
royal roads to original cooking with—
what you have on hand in the cupboard
or refrigerator

Written, illustrated and slightly abridged by Beverly Pepper

DOUBLEDAY & COMPANY, INC.
GARDEN CITY, NEW YORK

CONTENTS

"NOTHING IN THE HOUSE BUT——"

Note

Recipes for items followed by the letter *R* may be located by consulting the Index. The letter *S* after an item refers the reader to the "Substitute" that appears just below the ingredients.

INTRODUCTION

This is not a cookbook to shove any others off the shelf. It's not a rival to other cookbooks. It's a companion book to them—to all cookbooks in the world. It is written for people who can't bear to part with leftovers remaining from a previous meal, and for those who are tired of left-over hash and want to add to their cooking repertoire.

It is a book which starts out differently than any other cookbook. It begins with what you happen to have on hand and goes out from there—to satisfying and often magical solutions.

To put it in common terms, it is the answer to the age-old and frightened cry of "What'll we do now?" when you supposedly have nothing more in the house than a gang of hungry people piling in the front door.

When anybody tells me they hate leftovers, I recall a wonderful Chinese dinner I had some years ago. We were eight and were served *forty-three* different dishes at one sitting. Naturally, it was merely a small taste of each one. Then we were asked to determine the basis of all the various plates. No one agreed. At the end our hostess triumphantly announced she had served us only one thing—chicken cooked forty-three different ways.

That's leftovers for you.

It isn't a *problem* as much as the know-how of passing food from one form to the other.

It's both an exciting and economical passage. You have first of all the glamour of serving dull leftovers which have been magically transformed to bring you cheers and table-top kudos. And you have an amazing economy, too, of money and time.

It comes by itself, whenever you happen to have some leftovers and know how to use them. It comes even more when you *plan* on leftovers, both in buying and cooking.

It's a royal road to table romance. And as happens with romance, it changes everything. Once you start setting aside a little bit one day to create a leftover special for the next, you cease being a mere cook in the kitchen. You become, instead, a magician in the house—a priceless creator of table-top magic.

It sounds impossible? Actually it's very simple. Just tuck odds and ends back into the refrigerator, keep on hand a good supply of basic staples—and, suddenly, you're off!

Want an example?

Let's say you serve a pork roast, carefully putting aside a bit for later. To this bit you add green pepper, celery, and soy sauce and—presto!—it becomes pork chop suey! Or set aside some vegetables, say broccoli, and you find you can have a soufflé suitable as a main luncheon dish or perhaps an opening entree into a gourmet's evening.

Leftover recipes, like old friends, have another advantage. They're flexible to your needs. Proportions may vary with what's on hand. A little more or less meat, or vegetables, still achieves a comparable result. Frozen or fresh foods may also be substituted as long as you adjust for cooking time and liquid.

One last word on pantry staples. They are your tools and gadgets for kitchen magic. They are essential in the planned use of leftovers—or the emergency problem of "nothing in the house."

Staples mean sugar, salt, flour, onions, rice, potatoes, bouillon cubes, and a careful choice of canned items. For an ideal supply, note the Staple List. You save money and time if you keep it up to date.

With these and such free-wheeling ingenuity as we

have imprisoned between the covers of this book, there's no limit to what you can achieve on man or beast.

So that's it—whether you have one or a hundred cookbooks, this is a happy friend made to embrace a hundred books, a thousand leftovers, and a million moments of urgent necessity before the shifting tides of appetite which, like the sea itself, can at times call forth something of beauty and delight for man's pleasure, some incredibly tempting dish other than naked Venus on the half shell.

B. P.

STAPLE LIST

When buying staples, keep in mind you're setting up an emergency army. You're drafting accomplices and accessories for kitchen magic. Far from an unnecessary expense, they are the items which will save you three times their cost.

Most everyone has the below-listed items at one time or another. The trick is to keep them on hand all at one time. Check 'em once weekly, order what's lacking—and you're all set.

Remember to buy brands and sizes which fit your family and storage space. Large sizes, of course, are often more economical.

Include frozen foods if you've a freezer compartment in your refrigerator or a home freezer.

Almonds

Baking powder
Baking soda
Bouillon cubes or concentrates, beef and chicken

Canned foods: Breads; Fish: anchovies, crab meat, salmon, sardines, shrimp, tuna, etc.; Fruits; Juices; Meats and poultry; Sauces; Soups; Vegetables
Cereals and pastes: Macaroni, noodles, rice, spaghetti

Cheeses
Chocolate, unsweetened
Coffee, cocoa
Cooking wines, red, white, sherry
Condiments: Capers, horseradish, pickles, pimentos, red peppers, relishes
Corn meal
Cornstarch
Crackers

Desserts, gelatin and prepared
Dried beans, peas, and lentils

Dried fruits
Dried mushrooms

Flour

Herbs; dried: Basil, bay leaves, chives, garlic, marjoram, mint, parsley, saffron, sage, savory, tarragon, thyme

Jams, jellies, marmalades

Milk, evaporated and powdered

Mixes: Biscuit, cake, muffin, piecrust, etc.

Molasses, honey

Oil: Cooking, olive, salad
Olives, black, green, and stuffed

Peanut butter

Perishables: Bacon, butter, eggs, fat, lard, margarine

Salad dressing: French dressing, mayonnaise, etc.

Sauces: Catsup, chili, cocktail, soy, Tabasco, Worcestershire, etc.

Shortenings

Spices: Allspice, black pepper, cayenne pepper, celery salt, celery seed, chili powder, cinnamon, cloves, curry, garlic salt, ginger, mace, mustard, nutmeg, onion salt, paprika, poultry seasoning, sage, etc.

Sugar, brown, confectioner's

Tomato paste

Vinegar, herb, wine-flavored

MEATS

MEATS

Meat is the world's most desired food. Mistress of the kitchen and master of the dinner table, it's loved without caution or care around the world. Its proteins zip up energy without laying on fat. Its vitamins and minerals are great for the outside skin and inside heart. Since the heyday of the clumsy mastodon and lonely cave man, everybody has enjoyed its glorious benefits, as in the song, by eating "what comes naturally."

Like Proteus it pops up in a thousand forms and varieties. This makes for a simple solution for most anyone's taste except my mother-in-law, who's an old-time vegetarian—dreaming, on off days, I suspect, of a 3-inch, old-fashioned steak.

A surprising and little-known fact is that *meat's nutrition has no relation to its cost.* Tougher cuts have a nutritive value as high as the tender ones.

Meat is divided into two groups—red meats (beef or lamb) and white meats (pork, veal, etc.). Red meats may be served medium or rare, but the white must be well done, to be digestible in the delicate stomachs of our so-called Age of Anxiety.

A word about buying:

Buy by brand name when possible. And take a good look at the government stamp for wholesome quality. It says *U.S. Insp. and PS'D*—meaning *U.S. Inspected and Passed.* This is done by the meat packers and your government to protect you.

The cost of meat, basic factor in most any family's budget, makes it an ideal leftover target.

Buying long-cooking meats and planning for tomorrow, you save both fuel and meat costs. But do not buy such meats if you haven't time to do them justice—like the classic Frenchman, they simply won't be rushed.

The following leftovers are planned for your convenience. Wonderfully flexible, their proportions can vary with what's on hand. More or less meat or vegetables—or frozen or fresh foods—may be tossed in. Just make sure to adjust for cooking time and liquid.

Basic Cooking Instructions for Meat

BEEF

Beef Roast Wipe with damp cloth. Roast in shallow open pan. Rib roasts require no rack. Place rolled roasts on rack. Roast in slow 300° oven, fat side up, uncovered, without water. Do not baste. Cooking at low heat insures juicier meat and less shrinkage. If using meat thermometer, insert into center, through fat side; do not touch bone. Roasting time for standing *rib roasts* (6–8 lbs.): rare, 18–20 minutes per pound or 140° on meat thermometer; medium, 22–25 minutes per pound or 160° on thermometer; well done, 27–30 minutes per pound or 170° on thermometer. *Rolled rib roasts:* rare, 32 minutes per pound; medium, 38 min. per pound; well done, 48 minutes per pound. Or use thermometer as above. Season after roasting.

Beef Steak Broiling Have meat at room temperature. Wipe with damp cloth. Trim fat. Slash remaining fat every 2 inches to prevent curling when broiling. Rub preheated broiler rack with trimmed fat. For rare, cook thick steaks 3 inches below heat, 1-inch steaks 2 inches below. For well done, cook slower and further away. Turn with tongs; fork pierces meat, causes loss of juice. Season after broiling.

Beef Pot Roast Wipe with damp cloth. Brown slowly thoroughly on all sides in heavy kettle in little fat. For seasoning, add 1 each onion, carrot, potato—all finely diced, 2 or

3 peppercorns, salt and pepper, and ½ cup water (just enough to form steam). Simmer very slowly on rack, tightly covered. Turn meat twice. Cook until fork-tender (3–4 hours for 3–5 pound roast). Whole or quartered major vegetables, may be added ¾ hour before roast is done. If more water is needed, add ¼ cup boiling water at a time.

Beef Stew   Coat pieces with seasoned flour. Brown in fat in deep kettle, well and quickly on all sides. Add 1 cup boiling water; 1 each onion, carrot, potato—all finely diced; 2 or 3 peppercorns, bay leaf, sprig parsley, chopped celery stalk, dash of thyme, rosemary, and Worcestershire. Cover tightly. Cook very slowly until fork-tender, about 2 hours. Remove meat. Rub vegetables and stock through strainer, returning with meat to kettle. Add 1 cup boiling water and whole or quartered major vegetables. Cook very slowly until vegetables are tender, 30–45 minutes more.

LAMB

Lamb Roasts   Prepare as in Beef Roast instructions. Do not remove fell (thin paper-like covering)—it keeps meat in shape. Bone-in roasts take about 35 minutes per pound, or 175°–180° on the meat thermometer. Boned and rolled, (if stuffed, fill loosely) about 45 minutes per pound. See Beef Pot Roast instructions for pot roast (braised lamb), adding a bay leaf and 1 cup canned or cooked tomatoes, if you wish.

Lamb Crown Rib Roast   Be sure backbone is off or carving will be impossible. Remove ground meat, if any, and season well. Cover each rib bone with cubes of stale bread or salt pork to prevent burning. Replace seasoned ground meat or fill with stuffing. Add slivers of garlic if liked. Roast on rack in shallow pan in 300° oven about 30–35 minutes per pound.

Lamb Steaks and Chops   Thick meat is best broiled. Thin chops and steaks should be pan-broiled. Fell (paper-like covering) should be removed. To broil 2-inch chops, allow about 12 minutes each side. Chops 1 inch thick take about 6 minutes each side. Do not overcook. Should be juicy inside and brown outside. Breading makes small chops appear larger. Grease broiler rack with fat from meat. Turn with tongs.

Lamb Stew   Follow Beef Stew instructions, substituting juice and grated rind of 1 lemon for the Worcestershire. Curry goes well. So do peas and potatoes.

PORK AND HAM

Pork Roasts   Prepare as in Beef Roast instructions. Slivers of garlic may be inserted. Roast in 325°–350° oven. Pork must be thoroughly cooked with not a trace of pink left— 185° on meat thermometer. Roast fresh ham with rind on, removing when done. You may score surface in squares. Stick with cloves, sprinkle with brown sugar or honey, and brown in 400° oven 15 minutes.
Roast 8–10 pound fresh ham about 33 minutes per pound; 3–4 pound loin about 37 minutes per pound; 4–6 pound rolled shoulder roasts 45 minutes per pound; if stuffed, about 40 minutes.

Pork Crown Roast   Prepare like Lamb Crown Rib Roast. Roast in 350° oven, allowing 30–45 minutes per pound.

Pork Chops and Steaks   May be pan-fried or braised. Must be thoroughly cooked with no trace of pink. Remove excess fat, use to grease hot pan. Brown chops. Season. Cook covered or uncovered over low heat until well done, about 50 minutes. Turn occasionally.

Pork, Braised   Trim bit of fat and melt in heavy skillet. Sprinkle meat with salt, pepper, and flour. Brown well on both sides, about 10 minutes. Add boiling water or tomato juice, bouillon, sour cream, canned tomatoes, etc. Cook covered, simmering very slowly until tender and well done, about 50 minutes. Taste and season again if necessary.

To Bake Cured and Smoked Hams   Follow directions on wrapper. Bake in 300° oven. Ham, whole, 10–12 pounds,

25 minutes per pound, 170° on meat thermometer; 10–12 pounds tenderized, 15 minutes per pound or 160° on meat thermometer. Half ham, 6 pounds, 30 minutes per pound, 170° on meat thermometer. Tenderized, 15 minutes per pound, 160° on meat thermometer. Picnic hams, 3–10 pounds, 35 minutes per pound, 170° on meat thermometer. Remove rind after baking. Cut fat in squares. Dot with cloves, glaze with brown sugar or honey or apricot marmalade, etc. Brown in hot oven, 425° for 20 minutes.

Smithfield and Country Style Hams Require a thorough scrubbing and rinsing before soaking overnight in cold water to cover. Rinse, then add fresh cold water to cover. Simmer, allowing 30 minutes per pound. Remove rind, cut fat in squares, dot with cloves. Glaze and brown as above.

VEAL

Veal Roasts Roast veal in 300° oven. Leg, 7–8 pounds, 25–30 minutes per pound; shoulder, 7 pounds, 25–30 minutes per pound; shoulder, rolled, 5 pounds, 40–45 minutes per pound. All veal roasts should be well rubbed with fat or coated with strips of salt pork or bacon. Rub with flour, salt, and pepper if desired. Breast of veal requires 1 cup water in baking pan. All veal should be well done, 170° on meat thermometer.

Veal Pot Roasts Follow Beef Pot Roast instructions, but coat meat with flour before browning and add bay leaf and thyme to pot.

Veal Chops and Steaks Veal should never be broiled. Always add extra fat—butter, bacon, or fat salt pork. Rub meat with salt, pepper, and paprika. Good idea to give it a protective coating of either flour, bread crumbs, corn meal, etc., and/or dip into beaten egg and again into flour, etc. Brown slowly in butter, bacon drippings, or oil. Or braise in tomato juice, broth, water, etc. Always cook slowly. See Braised Pork for instructions. Undiluted cream soups make good sauces. Sliced lemon good with sautéed meat.

Veal Stew Follow Beef Stew, adding paprika and a can of tomato sauce. Cook 1½ hours or until fork-tender, then continue Beef Stew directions.

Leftover Meat

BEEF AND BROWN CELERY SAUCE

Leftover
BEEF STEW or ROAST, at least 1½ cups or 4 slices
and

Beef or bacon drippings, 3 tbsp.	Prepared horseradish, 1 tbsp.
Condensed celery soup, 1 can	Buttered bread crumbs, 2 tbsp.

Heat drippings in shallow casserole. Stir in celery soup until bubbly. Remove from heat. Add horseradish and beef slices. Top with buttered crumbs. Brown under broiler. MAKES 4 SERVINGS.

Suggested: Serve with noodles, Minted Peas in Onions[R], plus a salad of sliced radishes, fennel, and romaine lettuce with Piquante Dressing[R]—and Russian black bread.

BEEF BARBECUE

Leftover
BEEF ROAST, at least 2 cups in 1-inch cubes
and

Worcestershire sauce, ½ cup	Hamburger buns, 2–4
Catsup, ½ cup	Thinly sliced onion, 1 large
Dry mustard, ¼ tsp.	

Arrange beef in small, shallow baking dish. Combine Worcestershire, catsup, and mustard. Pour over meat. Make sure each piece is covered. Bake in moderate 375° oven about 45 minutes. Turn meat once or twice. Serve on split buns garnished with sliced onion. MAKES 4 SERVINGS.

Suggested: Serve with Delmonico Potatoes[R], pickles and relishes—wonderful with beer.

BEEF MIRONTON

Leftover
  BEEF STEW or ROAST, at least 4 slices or 1½ cups
  cut in small dice
and

Butter or margarine, 2 tbsp.	Bouillon, 1 cup or 1 cup meat stock
Thinly sliced yellow onions, 4	Red wine, ½ cup
Flour, 2 tbsp.	Salt and pepper to taste

Brown onions in butter. Blend in flour. Slowly pour in bouillon, stirring constantly, until thick and smooth. Add wine, salt, and pepper. Add the meat. Cover and simmer gently for 10 minutes. SERVES 2–3.

Suggested: Serve with boiled rice, Deep Fry Cauliflower[R], and head lettuce with French Dressing[R]—plus English muffins.

BEEF POTATO PIE

Leftover
  BEEF STEW or ROAST, at least 1½ cups, finely diced
and

Drippings, 3 tbsp.	Sliced mushrooms (optional), 1 4-ounce can
Diced onion, 1 large	
Chopped green pepper, 2 tbsp.	Worcestershire sauce, 1 tbsp.
Quick-frozen peas, 1 package or at least 1 cup cooked	Mashed potatoes, 2½ cups
	Butter or margarine, 1 tbsp.
	Milk, 2 tbsp.

Heat drippings in skillet. Add beef, onions, and green pepper. Cook until onions are soft. Add peas, mushrooms, and Worcestershire. Cook 5 minutes. Cover bottom of shallow casserole with half the mashed potatoes. (Add warm milk to potatoes if necessary to make them fluffy.) Pour on meat and vegetables. Cover with remaining mashed potatoes. Dot with butter, sprinkle with milk. Bake in medium hot 400° oven until golden brown, about 15 minutes. SERVES 3–4.

Suggested: Serve with Vegetable Macedoine Salad[R]— and rye bread.

BEEF STROGANOFF

Leftover
  STEAK or ROAST, at least 1½ cups cut into thin strips
and

Butter or margarine, 2 tbsp.	Sherry, 3 tbsp.
Sliced onions, 2 medium	Sour cream, ½–¾ cup
Sliced mushrooms, 1 can, drained	Salt and pepper to taste
Minced garlic, 1 clove	Worcestershire sauce, ½ tsp.
Flour, 1 tbsp.	Cooked, canned, or frozen vegetables (optional), any kind, 1 cup
Bouillon or consommé, ½ can condensed (do not dilute)	

Sauté onions and mushrooms with garlic in butter, until brown. Add lightly floured meat. Cook 1 minute. Remove meat and mushrooms. Blend flour into drippings. Pour in bouillon and sherry. Stir until smooth and thickened. Add sour cream, salt, pepper, and Worcestershire. Just before serving, add vegetables and return meat and mushrooms to pan.
Heat thoroughly. SERVES 2–3.

Suggested: Serve with Lima Bean Salad[R]—and pumpernickel bread.

CHINESE BEEF AND GREEN BEANS

Leftover
COOKED BEEF, cut into thin oblongs 1½ × 1 × ¼
inches, at least 1½ cups
and

Cornstarch, 2 tbsp.	Green pepper, cut in thin
Salt, ½ tsp.	strips, 1 small
Soy sauce, 1½ tbsp.	Cooked French string
Fat, 2 tbsp.	beans, 2 cups
Sliced white onion, 1	Sugar, 2 tbsp.
medium	Water, ⅔ cup
	Vinegar, 1 tablespoon

Combine ½ tbsp. cornstarch, salt, and 1 tbsp. soy sauce.
Pour over meat. Sauté meat in fat for 5 minutes. Add
onion and green pepper. Cook a few minutes. Add string
beans. Combine remaining cornstarch, soy sauce, sugar,
water, and vinegar. Pour over meat and vegetables.
Cook, stirring constantly until thickened. SERVES 3–4.

Variation: Add 4 sliced tomatoes to onion and green
pepper.

Suggested: Serve with boiled rice and fruit salad of
grapefruit slices, cut up strawberries, fresh mint on lettuce with lemon French Dressing[R].

CRUSTADE EGGS

Leftover
COOKED BEEF, finely chopped, at least 1 cup
and

Hard rolls, 4	Salt and pepper to taste
Hard-boiled eggs, 2	Tabasco, dash
Beaten egg, 1	Swiss cheese slivers, ¼ cup

Cut top off rolls. Scoop out all the crumbs. Chop eggs
finely with meat. Mix with beaten egg. Season with salt

and pepper. Add Tabasco. Fill scooped out rolls with the mixture. Top with cheese slivers. Cook under broiler until cheese has melted, about 6 minutes. MAKES 4 SERVINGS.

Suggested: Serve with Mixed Vegetable Scallop[R]—and iceberg lettuce wedges with Russian Dressing[R].

NEW ORLEANS GRILLADES

Leftover
    ROAST, at least 2 slices ½ inch thick
and

Butter or margarine, 1 tbsp.	Salt and pepper to taste
	Cayenne, dash
Chopped onion, 1 large	Bouillon or boiling water,
Chopped tomatoes, 1 cup	⅓ cup

Brown onion in hot butter. Add tomatoes, salt, pepper, and cayenne. Cook about 10 minutes. Add bouillon. Simmer another 10 minutes. Add meat slices and heat about 10 minutes more. SERVES 2.

Suggested: Serve with Vegetable Puffs[R] and individual Green Bean Salad Bowl[R]—and hot corn muffins.

SOUR CREAM BEEF RAGOUT

Leftover
    BEEF STEW or ROAST, at least 2 cups into 1-inch cubes
and

Beef drippings, 3 tbsp.	Sour cream, 2 cups
Flour, 3 tbsp.	Dill seed, 1 tsp.
Water, ½ cup	Salt, ¼ tsp.

Heat drippings in skillet. Add meat; blend in flour. Add water; stir until thick and smooth. Add sour cream, dill seed, and salt. Heat 1 minute more. SERVES 3-4.

Suggested: Serve with boiled noodles, Lyonnaise String Beans[R]—and toast triangles.

SOUTHERN SUCCOTASH AND
BEEF CHUNKS

Leftover
  STEAK or ROAST, cut in chunks, at least 2 cups
and

Oil, 1 tbsp.	Tomatoes, 1 cup
Chopped onion, 1	Caraway seeds, ½ tsp.
Succotash, 1 box frozen or 1 No. 2 can—or 1 cup kernel corn and 1 cup Lima beans	Salt and pepper to taste

Sauté onion in oil until lightly brown. Add meat, succotash, tomatoes, caraway seeds, salt, and pepper. Cover. Simmer slowly 25 minutes. SERVES 4.

Variation: Turn into buttered casserole, top with ¼ cup shredded cheese mixed with ¼ cup cracker crumbs. Bake in moderate 325° oven 30 minutes.

Suggested: Serve with a salad of endive, chopped celery, chopped apples, and French Dressing[R]—and hot biscuits.

STUFFED MEAT SLICES

Leftover
  ROAST, 4 slices ½ inch thick
and

Thinly sliced ham and/or Swiss cheese, 4 each	Flour, 1 tbsp.
Lightly beaten egg, 1	Bouillon, ½ cup—1 cube in ½ cup boiling water
Bread crumbs, ½ cup	Salt and pepper to taste
Butter or margarine, 3 tbsp.	Grated cheese (optional), 2 tbsp.

Cut a pocket into each meat slice. Place 1 slice ham and/or 1 slice cheese in each pocket. Close tightly and pin with toothpick. Dip into egg, then roll in bread crumbs. Fry in 2 tbsp. butter until brown. Remove. Add 1 tbsp. butter and flour to pan. Blend thoroughly. Add bouillon. Stir sauce until thickened. Season to taste. Return meat to pan. Sprinkle with cheese. Heat through and serve. SERVES 3–4.

Suggested: Serve with kidney beans, lettuce salad—and poppy-seed rolls.

SWISS STEAK AND KIDNEY BEANS

Leftover
BEEF ROAST, 2 slices 1½ inches thick
and

Flour, 4 tbsp.	Whole cloves, 2
Fat, 2 tbsp.	Salt to taste
Kidney beans, 1 No. 1 can	Red wine, or water, ¼ cup
Sliced onions, 2 medium	

Pound flour into both sides of meat slices. Brown in fat. Remove from skillet. Add kidney beans, onions, cloves, and salt. Cook until onions soften. Add meat and wine. Simmer *very gently* for 30 minutes. Do not boil or the meat will get tough. SERVES 2.

Suggested: Serve with Carrot Ramekins[R] and a mixed greens salad—with corn bread.

TAMALE PIE

Leftover
  COOKED BEEF, chopped, at least 1 cup
and

Corn meal, 1 cup	Tomatoes, 1 cup
Salt, 1½ tsp.	Thyme, ¼ tsp.
Boiling water, 4 cups	Chopped pimento, 2 tbsp.
Fat (drippings or shorten-ing), 2 tbsp.	Chili powder, 3 tsp.
	Dry mustard, ½ tsp.
Minced green pepper, 1 large	Chopped pimento olives, 2 tbsp.
Chopped onions, 2 small	Salt and pepper to taste
Corn kernels, 1 cup	Butter, 2 tbsp.

In top of double boiler, stir corn meal and salt slowly into boiling water. Continue stirring until thick. Place over boiling water, cook 20 minutes. Brown green pepper and onions in fat. Add corn, tomatoes, thyme, meat, pimento, chili powder, mustard, olives, salt, and pepper. Cook 5 minutes. Line shallow pan with half the corn meal. Pour in meat mixture. Cover with remaining corn-meal mixture. Dot with butter. Brown quickly in hot 425° oven 10 minutes. SERVES 2–3.

Suggested: Serve with sliced orange, thinly sliced onion, and endive salad—French Dressing[R]—and Italian bread sticks.

HAMBURGER SOUP

Leftover
  COOKED BEEF, ground, at least 1 cup
and

Grated onion, 1 tsp.	Slightly beaten egg white, 1, use just enough to moisten
Grated lemon rind, ½ tsp.	
Dried marjoram, ¼ tsp.	
Salt and pepper to taste	
Nutmeg, dash	Cream of chicken soup, bouillon, or what-have-you, at least 2 cups
Cracker crumbs, 2 tbsp.	

Mix meat (put through food chopper) with onion, lemon rind, marjoram, salt, pepper, nutmeg, and cracker crumbs moistened with egg white. Mix well, roll into walnut size balls. Cook 10 minutes in boiling soup. SERVES 2-3.

Suggested: Serve with Broccoli Soufflé Gourmet[R], crisp greens salad, and mayonnaise mixed with chopped olives —plus French bread.

KOFTA CURRY

Leftover
COOKED MEAT[S], put through the food chopper, at least 2 cups
and

Salt, ½ tsp.	Chili powder, pinch
Pepper, ¼ tsp.	Turmeric (optional), pinch
Grated onion, 2 tbsp.	
Mixed herbs, ½ tsp.	Ginger, pinch
Bread crumbs, 4 tbsp.	Minced garlic, ¼ tbsp.
Lightly beaten egg, 1	Water, 1 tbsp.
Butter or margarine or fat, ¾ tbsp.	Bouillon or hot water, 1 cup

Substitute: Fish or chicken.

Regrind meat with salt, pepper, grated onion, mixed herbs, and 1 tbsp. bread crumbs. Bind with egg. Shape into walnut-size balls and roll in remaining bread crumbs. Melt fat or butter in hot skillet. Add chili powder, turmeric, ginger, garlic, and 1 tbsp. water. Cook until slightly brown. Add meat balls and stir until evenly browned. Cover with bouillon or water and simmer gently for 45 minutes. SERVES 4.

Suggested: Serve with boiled rice, and a salad of sliced apples, oranges, onions marinated in French Dressing[R]— and rye bread.

MEAT-STUFFED PEPPERS

Leftover
  COOKED MEAT, diced finely, 1¼ cups
and

Firm green peppers, 4	Dry mustard, ½ tsp.
Beaten eggs, 2	Cayenne, dash
Milk, 1 cup	Chili powder (optional),
Salt, 1 tsp.	1 tbsp.
Pepper to taste	Buttered bread crumbs,
Grated onion, 1 small	4 tbsp.
Minced parsley, 1 tsp.	Boiling water, 1 cup

Cut tops from stem end of green peppers. Remove seeds and fibers. Parboil for 5 minutes. Drain. Prepare filling: mix eggs with milk, salt, pepper, onion, parsley, mustard, cayenne, and chili powder. Add meat. Fill peppers to within ½ inch of top. Sprinkle with bread crumbs. Place in baking dish filled with boiling water. Bake in moderate 350° oven until peppers are tender and filling is firm, about 40 minutes. MAKES 4 SERVINGS.

Suggested: Serve with Corn Chowder[R]—and hot buttered biscuits.

MULLIGATAWNY SOUP

Leftover
  COOKED MEAT, at least 2 cups, diced
and

Drippings, 3 tbsp.	salt, pepper and curry
Finely chopped onion, ¼ cup	powder, 1 tbsp.
Finely diced carrot, ¼ cup	Boiling water, 5 cups
Finely diced turnip, ¼ cup	Chopped parsley, 1 tbsp.
Peeled, diced green apples, 2 medium	Bay leaf, 1
Flour, 2 tbsp., mixed with	Thyme, ¼ tsp.
	Lemon juice, 1 tbsp.

Sauté onion, carrot, turnip and apples in drippings until almost tender—about 12 minutes. Add meat. Sprinkle with flour and curry mixture. Add water, parsley, bay leaf, and thyme. Simmer slowly, about 10 minutes. Add more pepper if desired. Add lemon juice just before serving. SERVES 4.

Suggested: Serve in hot soup bowls with a side dish of boiled rice—and Baked-Bean Burgers[R]—and soft rolls.

SWISS MEAT PIE

Leftover
  COOKED MEAT, put through food chopper, at least 1½ cups
and

Milk, ⅔ cup	Condensed mushroom soup, ½ can
Biscuit mix, 2 cups	
Bacon drippings, 2 tbsp.	Canned tomatoes, ⅔ cup, drained
Chopped onion, 1 small	
Salt, ½ tsp.	Swiss or American cheese, cut in slivers, ½ cup
Dry mustard, ½ tsp.	
Worcestershire sauce, 1 tsp.	

Prepare milk and biscuit mix for rolling as directed on package. Knead a few times. Set aside. Brown meat and onion in bacon drippings. Add salt, mustard, Worcestershire, soup, and tomatoes. Cook 10 minutes. Roll out biscuit dough and line 8-inch piepan. Fill with meat mixture. Cover with cheese. Bake in hot 450° oven 25 minutes until crust is done. SERVES 2–3.

Suggested: Serve with Asparagus and Olive Salad[R].

ZUCCHINI AND MEAT SAUCE

Leftover
COOKED HAMBURGER, at least 2 patties
and

Butter or margarine, 2 tbsp.	Bay leaf, 1
Flour, 2 tbsp.	Broth, bouillon, or stock, 2 tbsp.
Tomatoes, 1 cup	Salt and pepper to taste
Chopped green pepper, 2 tbsp.	Thinly sliced zucchini, 4 small
Chopped onion, 2 tbsp.	Grated cheese, 1 tbsp.
Basil, ¼ tsp.	

Chop hamburger finely. Melt butter. Blend in flour. Add tomatoes, green pepper, onion, basil, bay leaf, meat, and broth. Salt and pepper to taste. Simmer slowly about 10 minutes. Place sliced zucchini in shallow buttered baking dish. Cover with sauce, sprinkle with cheese. Bake in moderate 350° oven about 45 minutes. SERVES 2.

Suggested: Serve with Sweet-Potato Pie[R]—and toasted English muffins.

MEAT AND POTATO LATKES

Leftover
COOKED MEAT, ground, 2 cups
and

Grated raw potatoes, 2 cups	Eggs, 1 whole and 1 yolk
Minced onion, 1 tbsp.	Fat (shortening, lard, or salad oil) ¼ cup
Salt, ½ tsp.	Sour cream (optional), 1 cup
Pepper to taste	Tomato Sauce[R] or Cheese Sauce[R]
Worcestershire sauce, 1 tsp.	

Mix meat, potatoes, onion, salt, pepper, Worcestershire, and eggs. Form into flat round pancakes about ½ inch thick. Fry in fat until golden brown. Drain and serve with sour cream, Tomato or Cheese Sauce. SERVES 3–4.

Suggested: Serve with Cheese, Tomatoes, and Lima Beans[R].

NEAPOLITAN MEAT MACARONI

Leftover
COOKED MEAT, finely chopped, at least 1½ cups
and

Macaroni[S], ½ pound	Gravy, drippings, or
Boiling salted water, 2 quarts	strong bouillon, ½ cup
	Grated cheese, ¼ cup
Canned tomato sauce, 1 cup	

Substitute: Leftover spaghetti or macaroni. Rinse first with hot water. Drain; proceed as directed.

Boil macaroni in salted water until *al dente* (firm, not too soft). Mix the meat into the sauce and gravy. Sprinkle bottom of greased shallow casserole with 1 tbsp. grated cheese. Add layer of meat, then macaroni. Repeat cheese, meat, macaroni, etc., until used up. Top with cheese. Bake in hot 425° oven 7 minutes or until bubbling and browned. SERVES 3–4.

Variation: Slice 3 tomatoes ½ inch thick; sauté in 2 tbsp. butter and ¼ tsp. dried basil. Place on top of final macaroni layer. Top with cheese.

Suggested: Serve with salad of cooked string beans, broken romaine lettuce, crumbled bacon, and lemon French Dressing[R] plus—hot Italian garlic buttered bread.

SOUR-APPLE CASSEROLE

Leftover
  COOKED MEAT, diced, at least 1½ cups, or cut in 4–5 slices
and

Butter or margarine, 3 tbsp.	Sliced or diced, boiled potatoes, 4–5
Sliced onion, 1 large	Bouillon (cube and water) or meat stock, 1½ cups
Peeled and sliced sour apples, 2	Salt and pepper to taste
	Nutmeg, 1 pinch

Sauté onion and apples in butter until light brown. Place alternate layers of onion, apples, meat, and potatoes in shallow baking dish. Pour stock over all. Season with salt, pepper, nutmeg. Sprinkle with butter remaining in pan. Bake in moderate 350° oven 15–20 minutes. SERVES 3–4.

Suggested: Serve with a salad of canned or cooked diced beets, minced onions, minced green peppers, and Vinaigrette Dressing[R]—plus hot buttermilk biscuits.

STUFFED CABBAGE LEAVES

Leftover
  COOKED MEAT, any kind, put through the food grinder, about 1 cup
and

Finely chopped onion, 1	Beaten egg, 1
Parsley, 1 tbsp.	Cabbage leaves, 8
Bread crumbs, 2 tbsp.	Boiling salted water to cover
Thyme, pinch	
Marjoram, pinch	Bacon strips, 3
Caraway seeds, ¼ tsp.	White wine[s], ½ cup
Salt and pepper to taste	

Substitute: Chicken broth.

Mix meat with onion, parsley, bread crumbs, thyme, marjoram, caraway seeds, salt, and pepper. Blend in beaten egg. Choose perfect leaves from outside of cabbage. Parboil 5 minutes in salted water to cover. Drain and dry. Place a heaping spoonful of the mixture on each leaf. Fold two sides into mixture, flap one end over the other. Place bacon in bottom of shallow pan. Add the cabbage rolls. Cover with wine or broth; simmer gently 25 minutes. SERVES 4.

Suggested: Serve with boiled rice; cover with Tomato Sauce[R]—add a light salad—and Russian black bread.

VELOUTÉ MEAT TIMBALES

Leftover
COOKED MEAT, at least 1 cup, finely chopped or ground
and

Fat (shortening, lard, or drippings), 2 tbsp.	Sliced mushrooms (optional), 1 3-ounce can, drained
Flour, 2 tbsp.	Worcestershire sauce, 1 tsp.
Salt, 1 tsp.	
Concentrated beef or chicken stock, ½ cup	Finely chopped parsley, 1 tbsp.
Milk, ½ cup	
Well-beaten eggs, 2	

Melt fat, stir in flour and salt. Blend well. Add liquids gradually, stirring until thick and smooth. Remove from heat. Add eggs, mushrooms, Worcestershire, parsley, and meat. Mix well. Fill buttered custard cups ⅔ full. Place in pan of water. Bake in moderate 375° oven 25 minutes until set. Unmold. Serve with your favorite sauce. MAKES 4–5 TIMBALES.

Suggested: Serve with Macaroni Salad[R]—and hot buttered white toast.

SOUFFLÉ

Leftover
  COOKED MEAT, at least 1 cup, cut in small dice or
  chopped
and

Butter or margarine, 3 tbsp.	Milk, 1 cup
Flour, 3 tbsp.	Parmesan cheese, 3 tbsp.
Salt, ½ tsp.	Eggs, 3 yolks
Pepper, ¼ tsp.	Stiffly beaten egg whites, 3

Melt butter in a saucepan. Blend flour, salt, and pepper.
Add milk. Simmer, stirring constantly until thick and
smooth. Do not boil. Add meat and cheese. Remove from
heat. Stir in beaten egg yolks. Mix well. Fold in stiffly
beaten egg whites. Pour into buttered soufflé dish. Bake
in moderate 375° oven 25 minutes. Serve at once. SERVES
3-4.

Suggested: Serve with Minted Carrot and Chicory Salad[R]
—and popovers.

EGG CROQUETTES

Leftover
  COOKED MEAT, or FISH, or POULTRY, at least ½ cup,
  finely chopped
and

Butter or margarine, 1 tbsp.	Chopped parsley, 1 tsp.
Eggs, 3	Flour, ½ cup
Salt, ½ tsp.	Bread crumbs, ½ cup
Pepper, dash	Oil or fat, ¼ cup
Milk or cream, ¼ cup	White sauce (Béchamel
Grated onion, 1 tsp.	Medium[R])

Melt butter in skillet. Beat 2 eggs with salt, pepper, and
milk until frothy. Pour into skillet. Stir constantly until

just beginning to set. Stir in chopped meat, fish, or chicken. Add onion and parsley. Mix well. Remove from heat. Cool. Shape into 4 croquettes. Beat remaining egg. Roll mixture in egg, then in flour, again in the egg, then in bread crumbs. Fry in fat or oil, turning until evenly browned. Drain on absorbent paper. Serve with white sauce. MAKES 4 CROQUETTES.

Variation: Rolled into small walnut-size balls, fried, and served on toothpicks, you have a fine hors d'oeuvre.

STUFFED ZUCCHINI

Leftover
COOKED MEAT, at least ¾ cup, very finely chopped
and

Zucchini, 8 small	Olive oil, 1 tbsp.
Parsley (optional), 2 tsp.	Butter or margarine,
Lightly beaten egg, 1	1 tbsp.
Grated cheese (optional), 2 tbsp.	Lard, 1 tbsp.
	Chopped onion, 1 small
Nutmeg, dash	Minced garlic, 1 clove
Salt and pepper to taste	Tomato paste, 2 tbsp.
Bread crumbs, 1½ tbsp.	Water or bouillon, 1 cup

Halve zucchini lengthwise. Remove insides carefully with an apple corer or a small paring knife. Take care not to break the skin. Mix together the meat, parsley, egg, cheese, nutmeg, salt, and pepper. Add bread crumbs. Mix again. Stuff zucchini halves with the mixture. Melt the oil, butter, and lard in a large skillet. Brown the onion and garlic in this mixture. Add tomato paste diluted with the water or bouillon. Cook a few minutes. Add the stuffed zucchini. Cook tightly covered over low heat, until tender, about 25 minutes. Add a little hot water if necessary. MAKES 16 STUFFED ZUCCHINI HALVES.

Suggested: Serve with buttered sweet corn—and hot cross buns.

BIDDLEFORD PIE

Leftover
BAKED HAM, at least 2 cups, diced
and

Butter or margarine, 2 tbsp.	Diced, cooked or canned potatoes, 1 cup
Flour, 2 tbsp.	Cooked or defrosted frozen peas, 1 cup
Milk, ½ cup	
White wine, ½ cup	Thyme, ½ tsp.
Salt and pepper to taste	Biscuit mix, 2 cups
Drained oysters, 1½ cups	Milk, 1 cup

Melt butter; stir in flour. Blend well. Add milk and wine gradually, stirring until thick and smooth. Add salt, pepper, oysters, ham, potatoes, peas, and thyme. Pour into shallow buttered baking dish. Mix biscuit mix with milk. Spread over ham and oyster mixture. Bake in moderate 350° oven 30 minutes. SERVES 4.

Suggested: Serve with chicory and tomato salad with Mustard Dressing[R].

HAM AND GREEN NOODLES

Leftover
COOKED HAM, at least 1½ cups, cut in long, narrow strips
and

Olive oil, 1 tbsp.	Bouillon, 1½ cups
Minced onion, 3 tbsp.	Salt and pepper to taste
Minced garlic, 1 clove	Green noodles, ½ pound
Minced parsley, 1 tsp.	Boiling water, 3 quarts
Minced carrot, 2 tbsp.	Grated Parmesan cheese,
Tomato paste, 1 tbsp.	4 tbsp.

Brown ham, onion, garlic, parsley, and carrot in oil. Add tomato paste mixed with bouillon. Simmer gently 10 minutes. Taste for seasoning. Cook noodles in salted water until *al dente* (firm, not too soft). Serve on hot platter, ham in center, sauce poured over all. Sprinkle with grated cheese. SERVES 3–4.

Suggested: Serve with cottage cheese salad, Cucumber Dressing[R], red wine—and hot rolls.

HAM AND LIMA CASSEROLE

Leftover
  COOKED HAM, ground, at least 1 cup
and

  Cooked, frozen, or defrosted Lima beans, 1½ cups
  Bread crumbs, ½ cup
  Prepared mustard, ¾ tsp.
  Horseradish, ½ tsp.

  Salt and pepper to taste
  Milk, 1 cup
  Sliced tomatoes, 2 medium
  Melted butter or margarine, 3 tsp.

Combine Lima beans, bread crumbs, mustard, horseradish, salt, pepper, and milk. Place ham in bottom of buttered baking dish. Spread Lima mixture over it. Top with layer of sliced tomatoes. Sprinkle with melted butter. Bake in moderate 350° oven 40 minutes. SERVES 2–3.

Suggested: Serve with a salad of sliced avocado, marinated in French Dressing[R], on salad greens garnished with sliced olives—and hot buttered rolls.

HAM AND SCALLOPED SWEETS

Leftover
   COOKED HAM, at least 1½ cups, diced
and

Thinly sliced cooked sweet potatoes[s], 4	Butter or margarine, 1½ tbsp.
Flour, 2 tbsp., mixed with 1 tsp. salt and pepper to taste	Milk, 1½ cups

Substitute: Raw potatoes. Follow same directions, but bake in moderate 375° oven 1 hour until potatoes are done.

Place a layer (about 1 cup) of potatoes in small buttered casserole. Sprinkle with 1 tbsp. seasoned flour. Top with ¾ cup ham. Cover with another cup sliced potatoes, repeat ham, and then remaining potatoes. Sprinkle with remaining tablespoon flour. Dot with butter. Pour milk over all. Bake in medium hot 400° oven 30 minutes—until top is well browned. SERVES 2–3.

Suggested: Serve with Curried Pea Spoon-Fritters[R]—omit curry if desired—and French bread.

JELLIED HAM SALAD

Leftover
   COOKED HAM[s], diced, at least 1½ cups
and

Unflavored gelatin, 1 envelope softened in ¼ cup cold water	Romaine lettuce
	Pared sliced avocado, 1
Mayonnaise, 1½ cups	American cheese slivers, ⅔ cup
Chopped hard-cooked eggs, 2	French dressing (2 parts oil to one part vinegar, salt and pepper to taste)
Cooked asparagus tips, cut in 1-inch lengths, 1 cup	
Chopped chives, 1 tbsp.	

Substitute: Cooked chicken.

Place gelatin and cold water in top of double boiler. Heat over boiling water until gelatin dissolves. Remove from heat. Stir in mayonnaise. Add eggs, asparagus tips, chopped chives, and ham. Pour into ring mold. Chill until set. Unmold on bed of crisp romaine lettuce. Fill center with sliced avocado and American cheese. Serve with French dressing. MAKES A MAIN-COURSE SALAD FOR 4.

Suggested: Serve with either corn fritters or squash soufflé—and hot buttermilk biscuits.

MACARONI MILANESE

Leftover
  COOKED HAM and/or TONGUE, cut in thin strips, enough to make at least 1 cup
and

Macaroni, ½ pound	Sliced mushrooms
Boiling salted water, 3 quarts	(optional), 1 4-ounce can
Red wine, 1 cup	Salt and pepper to taste
Tomato sauce, 1 cup	Butter, 1 tbsp.
Tomato juice[S], 1 cup	Grated cheese, 4 tbsp.

Substitute: Bouillon cube and water.

Boil macaroni in salted water until almost cooked, about 10 minutes. It should be soft but underdone. Place wine, tomato sauce, tomato juice, ham, and/or tongue, mushrooms, salt and pepper, in a saucepan. Simmer 10 minutes. Add drained macaroni. Cook another 10 minutes. Correct seasoning. Serve topped with butter sprinkled with cheese. SERVES 2–3.

Suggested: Serve with Green Bean Salad Bowl[R]—and Italian garlic bread.

BAGDAD CASSEROLE

Leftover

COOKED LAMB, at least 1½ cups cut in small dice

and

Diced, cooked or raw eggplant, at least 1 cup	Cooked rice, 2 cups
Oil, ¼ cup	Tomatoes, 1 No. 1 can, drained, or 1 cup fresh
Minced onion, ½ cup	Red wine, ½ cup
Chopped green pepper, ¼ cup	Grated cheese, ½ cup
Garlic, 1 clove	Salt and pepper to taste

If using raw eggplant, cook until tender. Drain well. Sauté onion, green pepper, and garlic in oil. Remove garlic. Add lamb, rice, eggplant, tomatoes, wine, ¼ cup cheese, salt, and pepper to taste. Turn into earthenware casserole. Top with remaining cheese. Bake in medium hot 400° oven about ¾ hour. SERVES 2–3.

Suggested: Serve with a salad of grated raw carrots, seedless raisins, raw celery on curly endive with French Dressing[R]—and hot drop biscuits.

INDIAN PILAF

Leftover

COOKED LAMB or BEEF or CHICKEN, cut in 1½-inch lengths, about 1½ cups

and

Butter or margarine, 2 tbsp.	Mace, pinch
Coarsely chopped onions, 1 cup	Cloves, 2 or 3
Crushed garlic, 1 clove	Ginger, pinch
Raw rice, 1 cup	Salt and pepper to taste
Chopped almonds, 1 tbsp.	Saffron, pinch
Raisins, 2 tbsp.	Hot chicken stock, 2 cups
Cinnamon, ¼ tsp.	Hard-boiled eggs (optional), 2

Sauté onions and garlic in butter until golden brown. Remove garlic. Add meat, rice, almonds, raisins, cinnamon, mace, cloves, ginger, salt, and pepper. Stir in saffron and chicken stock. Cook covered with heavy lid very slowly until rice is tender and each grain is separated from the other—about 18 minutes. Garnish with sliced hard-boiled eggs if liked. SERVES 3–4.

Suggested: Serve with Almond Spinach Croquettes[R] plus one half recipe for Mixed Beet Ring Mold[R]—and French bread.

LAMB ROLL

Leftover
COOKED LAMB, at least 1½ cups, ground
and

Biscuit mix, 1 cup	Chopped parsley, 1 sprig
Milk, ⅓ cup	Chopped pimento olives,
Butter or margarine,	2 tbsp.
1 tbsp.	Dry mustard, ½ tsp.
Minced onion, 1 small	Relish, 2 tbsp.
Cream of mushroom soup,	Salt and pepper to taste
1 can	

Prepare biscuit mix with milk as directed for rolled biscuits on package. Set aside on waxed paper. Brown onion in butter. Add ½ can mushroom soup, lamb, parsley, olives, mustard, relish, salt, and pepper. Cook slowly 10 minutes. Roll out biscuit dough to 8 × 4-inch rectangle. Spread with mixture. Roll like jelly roll. Seal edges with dampened fingers. Brush with milk. Bake in hot 425° oven 30 minutes, or until done. Cut in four slices with sharp knife. Serve with remaining hot soup or hot leftover gravy and mint jelly. SERVES 4.

Variation: Try substituting ½ cup cooked dried apricots for the olives, relish, parsley, and mustard.

Suggested: Serve with buttered broccoli, plus individual salads of cottage cheese, watercress, and sliced tomatoes.

CHINESE PORK AND PEPPERS

Leftover

COOKED PORK SHOULDER or ROAST PORK, cut
into strips 1½ inch long, ¼ inch wide, at least 1½ cups
and

Salad oil or fat, 2 tbsp.	Diced green peppers, 3
Salt, ½ tsp.	medium
Chicken bouillon cube, 1	Slivered celery, 1 cup
dissolved in 1½ cups	Cornstarch, 2 tbsp.
boiling water	Cold water, ¼ cup
Soy sauce, 2 tbsp.	Black molasses or honey,
	2 tbsp.

Brown meat in hot oil. Sprinkle with salt; add bouillon
and soy sauce. Bring to boil. Reduce heat; simmer 5 minutes. Add peppers and celery; mix well. Bring to boil.
Reduce heat; cook 10 minutes. Mix cornstarch with water. Add molasses. Stir until smooth. Add to pork and
vegetables. Stir for another few minutes until thickened.
SERVES 2–3.

Suggested: Serve with fried rice, crisp canned Chinese
noodles, and a salad of diced pineapple chunks and
grated raw cranberries with lemon French Dressing[R] on
lettuce cups.

DANISH PANCAKE

Leftover

ROAST PORK, 4–8 thin slices
and

Fat or oil, 2 tbsp.	Milk, ½ cup
Well-beaten eggs, 3	Salt and pepper to taste
Flour, 2 tbsp.	Chopped chives, 2 tbsp.

Heat fat in skillet. Add pork slices, brown quickly. Remove from pan. Drain off excess fat, leaving only a thin

surface coating. Mix eggs, flour, and milk. Season with salt and pepper. Pour mixture into skillet. Cook over low heat until bottom is set and top still creamy. Add pork slices. Sprinkle with chives. Cover. Cook a few minutes until set. SERVES 3–4.

Suggested: Serve with Mashed Potato Cheese Balls[R] and a salad of canned pear halves and diced orange on watercress with French Dressing[R]—plus hot cross buns.

FANTASTIC BELGIAN MEAT BALLS

Leftover
COOKED PORK, put through meat grinder, at least 1½ cups

and

Butter or margarine, 1 tbsp.	Flour, ½ cup
Chopped shallot, 1	Butter or margarine, 3 tbsp.
Bread slices, 2 soaked in ½ cup milk seasoned with: salt, pepper, and nutmeg to taste	Tiny onions, 12
	Scraped new potatoes, 12
	Chopped parsley, 1 tsp.
	Thyme, ¼ tsp.
White wine, 3 tbsp.	Bay leaf, 1
Egg yolk, 1	Stock, white wine, or light beer, 1 cup
Stiffly beaten egg white, 1	

Brown shallots in butter. Mix with meat, soaked bread, wine, egg yolk. Blend well. Fold in egg white. Shape into small balls. Roll in flour. Heat butter in skillet. Add meat balls; brown quickly. Add onions and potatoes. Sprinkle with parsley. Add thyme and bay leaf. Cover with wine, beer, or stock. Simmer covered about 35 minutes until potatoes are done. SERVES 3–4.

Suggested: Serve with tomato and watercress salad, French Dressing[R]—and French bread.

FESTA PORK AND RICE

Leftover
ROAST PORK, at least 4 ¼-inch-thick slices
and

Oil, 2 tbsp.	Tomato sauce, 1 8-ounce can
Sliced onions, 2 medium	
Crushed garlic, 1 clove	Sliced mushrooms (optional), 1 3-ounce can, undrained
Sliced green pepper (optional), 1	
Gravy, 1 cup—or ½ can beef gravy	Minced parsley, 1 tsp.
	Salt and pepper to taste
	Raw rice, 1 cup

Brown onions, garlic, and green pepper in oil in heavy skillet. Add gravy, tomato sauce, mushrooms, parsley, and seasonings. Simmer uncovered 15 minutes. Measure sauce. If necessary add boiling water or bouillon to make 2¼ cups. Check seasoning. Reserve 2 tbsp. sauce. Mix in rice. Place half the meat slices on bottom of earthenware casserole. Top with half the rice and sauce combination. Add remaining pork slices, then the rest of the rice and sauce. Spread with reserved sauce. Bake covered in 400° oven about 1 hour until rice is tender. SERVES 4.

Suggested: Serve with hot buttered peas, heart of lettuce salad, Blue Cheese Dressing[R]—and poppy-seed rolls.

PORK CHOP SUEY

Leftover
COOKED PORK, at least 1½ cups cut into thin strips
and

Dried mushrooms, 4–5 tbsp. (1 ounce)	Bean sprouts (optional), 1 can
Hot water, 2 cups	Finely diced celery, 1 cup
Salad oil, 1 tbsp.	Bouillon, 1 cube dissolved in ¾ cup water
Soy sauce, 3 tbsp.	
Green pepper, cut in strips, ½ cup	Flour or cornstarch, 2 tbsp.
	Egg, 1

Soak mushrooms in hot water 15 minutes. Drain. Heat oil with 1 tbsp. soy sauce. Add green pepper, bean sprouts, mushrooms, celery. Cook another minute. Add bouillon. Simmer 10 minutes. Blend flour or cornstarch with 2 tbsp. soy sauce. Stir into above. Heat until thickened. Beat egg; fry in lightly oiled pan. Cut into strips. Serve as garnish for chop suey. SERVES 3–4.

Suggested: Serve with boiled rice, canned crisp Chinese noodles, and canned litchi nuts.

PORK WITH HORSERADISH

Leftover
COOKED PORK, cut in 2-inch slivers, at least 2 cups
and

Sliced onions, 3 medium	Bay leaf, 1
Fat or salad oil, 2 tbsp.	Salt and pepper to taste
Stock or bouillon, ½ cup	Horseradish, 2 tbsp.
Wine vinegar, ¼ cup	Croutons

Sauté onions in fat. Add pork. Cover with stock and vinegar. Add bay leaf, salt, and pepper. Simmer uncovered 20 minutes. Serve sprinkled with horseradish and garnished with croutons. SERVES 4.

Suggested: Serve on mashed potatoes and Mushroom Croquettes[R] plus a lettuce and sour grass salad with lemon French Dressing[R]—and pumpernickel bread.

PORK AND YAM POT

Leftover

COOKED PORK or HAM, at least 1½ cups, cut in cubes

and

Sliced apples, ¾ cup

Cooked peas, or defrosted frozen, 1 cup

Pared and sliced, cooked sweet potatoes, 4 medium

Salt and pepper to taste

Gravy or brown sauce, 1 cup

Cinnamon, ¼ tsp.

Bread crumbs, 2 tbsp.

Butter or margarine, 3 tsp.

Arrange pork, apples, peas, and potatoes in alternate layers in earthenware casserole. Season with salt and pepper. Pour over gravy. Sprinkle with cinnamon mixed with bread crumbs. Dot with butter. Bake in moderate 350° oven about 40 minutes. SERVES 2–3.

Suggested: Serve with a salad of sliced oranges and raw onions marinated in French Dressing[R] and tossed with Boston lettuce—plus Parker House rolls.

SWEET AND SOUR SPARERIBS

Leftover
  BROILED SPARERIBS, at least 2 cups, cut into 2-inch pieces
and

Butter, margarine, or salad oil, 2 tbsp.	Pineapple juice, ⅓ cup
Sliced onion, 1 large	Water, 3 tbsp.
Brown sugar, 3 tbsp.	Salt, ¼ tsp.
Vinegar, ¼ cup	Pepper to taste
Soy sauce, 1 tsp.	Cornstarch, 1 tsp.
	Water, 1 tsp.

Sauté onion in butter, margarine, or salad oil. Add sugar, vinegar, soy sauce, pineapple juice, water, salt, pepper, and spareribs. Simmer slowly 20 minutes. Mix cornstarch with cold water, add to sauce, stir until boiling. Simmer slowly 10 minutes. SERVES 2.

Variation: Add pineapple chunks.

Suggested: Serve with boiled rice mixed with handful of chopped parsley—plus torn iceberg lettuce salad with French Dressing[R] and Italian bread sticks.

HUNGARIAN GOULASH

Leftover
  COOKED VEAL or BEEF, cut in 1-inch cubes, at least 1½ cups
and

Paprika, 2 tbsp.	Tomato paste, 1 tbsp.
Olive oil, or very good salad oil, 2 tbsp.	Consommé, 1 can—or 2 chicken bouillon cubes in 2 cups water
Finely chopped onions, 4 medium	Caraway seeds, ¼ cup
Garlic, 1 clove	Salt and pepper to taste

Remove any bone and fat from meat. Rub each piece thoroughly with paprika. Sauté the onions and garlic in the oil until golden brown. Add the meat and cook 5 minutes. Add tomato paste, consommé, caraway seeds, salt, and pepper. Simmer slowly 20 minutes. This is wonderful with black bread. SERVES 2–3.

Suggested: Serve with broad egg noodles and a salad of cucumber, escarole, and mustard greens with French Dressing[R].

ROSSINI VEAL BIRDS

Leftover
    COOKED VEAL, 2–4 slices, cut in thin slices 4 inches square
and

Bread crumbs, 1 cup—soaked in ½ cup red wine

Anchovy fillets, 2—or anchovy paste, ½ tsp.

Finely chopped parsley, onion, capers, 1 tsp. each

Basil, ⅛ tsp.

Well-beaten egg, 1

Salt and pepper to taste

Olive oil, butter, or margarine, 1 tbsp.

Dry red wine, ½ cup

Pitted black olives (optional), ½ cup

Squeeze wine from bread crumbs. Mix crumbs with anchovies, parsley, onion, capers, basil, egg, salt, and pepper. Spread some of the mixture on each slice of veal. Roll each and tie with string or secure with toothpick. Heat oil or butter, add veal "birds." Pour on wine. Cook covered over low heat until wine evaporates. Serve garnished with black olives. SERVES 2.

Suggested: Serve with polenta (corn-meal mush), raw spinach and bacon salad with French Dressing[R]—plus Italian bread.

SPANISH VEAL CUTLETS

Leftover
COOKED VEAL, at least 2 slices
and

Fat or oil, 1 tbsp.	Pounded almonds or
Chopped onion, 1 small	mixed nuts, 1 tbsp.
White wine, ½ cup	Grated chocolate, ½ tsp.
Tomato purée, 3 tbsp.	Saffron, pinch
Stock, 3 tbsp.	Salt and pepper to taste
Canned sliced mushrooms,	Boiled ham, size of veal
2 tbsp.	pieces, 2 slices

In skillet, sauté onion in fat until golden. Drain off fat; add wine, tomato purée, and stock. Simmer gently for 5 minutes. Add the mushrooms, nuts, chocolate, saffron, salt, and pepper. Simmer another few minutes. Add the cutlets and ham. Heat thoroughly. Place the cutlets on heated serving dish. Top with the ham and sauce. SERVES 2.

Suggested: Serve with brown rice and salad of dandelion greens with French Dressing[R] pepped up with a few dashes of Tabasco—plus Italian bread.

VEAL PAPRIKA

Leftover
COOKED VEAL, 4 slices, or cut in chunks, at least 1 cup
and

Fat, 2 tbsp.	Flour, ¼ cup
Sliced onions, 2	Salt and pepper to taste
Paprika, 1 tbsp.	Sour cream, 1 cup

Sauté onions in hot fat until brown. Sprinkle with paprika. Coat veal with flour. Add to onions. Cook 5 minutes over low heat. Add salt, pepper, and sour cream. Cook another few minutes. SERVES 2.

Suggested: Serve with elbow macaroni and mixed field

salad, sour grass, and iceberg lettuce—caraway seeds in French Dressing[R]—plus rye bread.

BEHAR RICE AND KIDNEYS

Leftover
 COOKED KIDNEYS, thinly sliced, at least 1½ cups
and

Butter or margarine, 5 tbsp.	Sliced onions, 2 medium
	Tomato paste, 2 tbsp.
Raw rice, 1 cup	Parsley, 2 tbsp.
Boiling bouillon or stock, 2 cups	Boiling water or bouillon, 1¼ cups
Salt, ½ tsp.	Salt and pepper to taste
Fat, 2 tbsp.	

Melt 2 tbsp. butter in heavy skillet. Stir in rice and keep stirring over low heat 5 minutes. Add 2 cups bouillon and salt. Cover very tightly. Simmer gently for about 20 minutes, until done. Remove to deep casserole. Top with remaining 3 tbsp. butter. Bake in moderate oven until top is brown. Brown onions in fat. Add kidneys, tomato paste, parsley, water, salt, and pepper. Simmer slowly for 10 minutes. SERVES 3.

Suggested: Serve with carrot fritters, torn spinach and bacon salad with garlic French Dressing[R]—plus hot buttered biscuits.

EGGS POULETTE

Leftover
COOKED LIVER, diced, at least 1 cup
and

Butter or margarine, 2 tbsp.	Eggs, 4–8
Sherry, 1 tbsp.	Salt, ½ tsp.
Buttered bread crumbs, 3 tbsp.	Pepper, ¼ tsp.

Brown liver in butter. Add sherry. Cook 5 minutes. Sprinkle 1 tsp. buttered bread crumbs in bottom of each of 4 shirred-egg dishes (or ramekins or custard cups). Break 1 or 2 eggs into each dish and sprinkle with salt and pepper. Circle with livers, finely chopped; top with remaining buttered bread crumbs. Bake in moderate 325° oven 15 minutes or until eggs are set. MAKES 4 SERVINGS.

Suggested: Serve with hashed brown potatoes, cauliflower in Mustard Sauce^R—and tiny hard rolls.

VARIETY MEAT BARBECUE

Leftover
COOKED LIVER or KIDNEY or HEART or SWEETBREAD, enough of any one or a combination to make at least 1½ cups, cut in 1-inch pieces
and

Butter or margarine, 1 tbsp.	Parsley, ½ tsp.
Flour, 1½ tbsp.	Thyme, pinch
Stock, 1 cup	Chopped onion, 1
Capers, 1 tbsp.	Grated rind of 1 lemon
Chopped anchovies, 1 tbsp.	Lemon juice, 1 lemon
Vinegar, 1 tbsp.	Lump sugar, 2 lumps
	Salt and pepper to taste
	Parker House rolls, 3–4

Melt butter in saucepan. Blend flour gradually, stirring until light brown. Add stock slowly, stirring constantly until thick and smooth. Mix in capers, anchovies, vinegar, parsley, thyme, onion, lemon rind, lemon juice, sugar, salt, and pepper. Mix well. Add meat. Simmer a few minutes. Serve on hot scooped out Parker House rolls. SERVES 3–4.

Suggested: Serve with Vegetable Macedoine Salad[R].

TONGUE CASSEROLE

Leftover
   COOKED TONGUE, at least 8 slices cut ¼ inch thick *and*

Tomatoes, ½ cup	Sugar, ⅓ cup
Sliced white onion, 1 medium	Butter or margarine, 2 tbsp.
Vinegar, ¼ cup	Cinnamon, ¼ tsp.
Tongue stock (or bouillon), ½ cup	Cloves, ⅛ tsp.
	Salt, ½ tsp.

Mix all ingredients together in saucepan. Simmer 15 minutes. Place tongue in shallow casserole. Cover with sauce. Bake 35–40 minutes in moderate 350° oven. SERVES 2–3.

Suggested: Serve over fluffy boiled rice or with tiny new potatoes. Add mixed greens and green bean salad with French Dressing[R]—and Russian black bread.

ZUPPA DI PAPA'

Leftover
  SAUSAGE, at least 2, cut in 1-inch pieces
and

Lard, 1 tbsp.
Finely chopped onion, 1
Finely chopped celery, 1
  tsp.
Finely chopped parsley,
  1 tsp.
Tomato paste, 1 tbsp.
Salt, ¼ tsp.
Tiny red pepper, 1 pod—
  or coarse black pepper
  to taste

Well-beaten eggs
  (optional), 2
Bouillon cubes or
  concentrate, 2–3
  dissolved in 5 cups
  boiling water
Stale or toasted bread, 4
  slices—rubbed with cut
  garlic

Brown onion, celery, and parsley with sausage in lard. Add tomato paste, salt, and pepper. Remove from heat. Stir in eggs. Pour bouillon over all. Boil covered 10 minutes. Place 1 slice of bread in each soup plate. Pour soup over bread slices. SERVES 3–4.

Suggested: Serve with Eggplant Parmesan[R] and mixed greens salad with French Dressing[R]—and toasted rye bread.

FISH

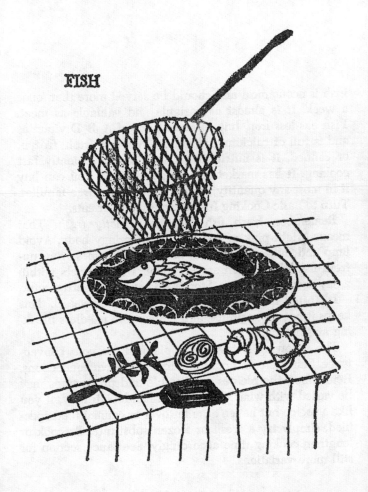

FISH

Fish is economical and should be served more than once a week. It is almost as variable and valuable as meat. Fish has less iron, but an abundance of A–B–D vitamins and is full of calcium and iodine. Whether fresh, frozen, or canned, it is nutritious as well as conveniently fast cooking. It has market advantages as well. You can buy it in most any quantity, for either small or large families. Turn to Basic Cooking Instructions for short cuts.

Remember, fresh fish must be *strictly fresh*. That means bright pink or red gills, firm springy body. Avoid limp and dull-eyed fish. A "fishy" smell comes from unfresh fish. Frozen fish are excellent. Use leftovers within a day or two—not more. Store well covered in refrigerator.

It's often best to cook fish in its serving vessel. This keeps it hot, looks pretty, and helps avoid needless breaking and flaking.

The following leftovers are planned for your convenience. Start here and continue into your own concoctions. Remember, the recipes are flexible and proportions may be varied with what you have on hand. Naturally, if you like a recipe but haven't the leftover or canned food specified, simply try a fresh or frozen substitute. Precook or lengthen cooking time accordingly. See sauce section for still more variations.

Basic Cooking Instructions for Fish

Baked Split Whole Fish Buy fish with scales and viscera removed. Save head for fish stock, chowder, or gravy.

Have fish split. Brush all sides with melted butter, oil, or fat. Season with salt and pepper and paprika. Squeeze over a little lemon juice or tarragon vinegar. Bake skin side down on greased shallow baking dish in moderate 325° oven until done, about 45 minutes for a 4-pound fish. The fish is done as soon as the flesh is opaque and will flake when tried with a fork. Baste occasionally with melted butter or vegetable liquid.

Baked Stuffed Whole Fish   Dust inside and out with salt and pepper. Stuff lightly with desired stuffing, making it no more than ½ inch thick. Sew opening or close with toothpicks and string. Dot with butter or oil or cover with strips of bacon or fat salt pork. Bake in shallow greased baking dish, uncovered, in moderate 325° oven about 45 minutes or until done, test as above. Baste after first 10 minutes with vegetable juices, or equal parts white wine and water.

Baked Fish Fillets and Steaks   Brush fish generously with melted butter, oil, or savory fat. Sprinkle with salt, pepper, and lemon juice; and/or dip in salted milk, roll in crumbs seasoned with pepper. Bake in shallow greased baking dish in moderate 325° oven until flesh will flake when tried with fork. Do not turn. Good with tomato, cheese, hollandaise or cream sauce. Lemon wedges always welcome.

Baked Stuffed Fish Steaks   If steak is too thick, cut in half lengthwise. Dust each with salt and pepper. Place stuffing between 2 steaks, sandwich fashion. Brush top with oil or dot with butter or bacon bits, melted butter or bacon drippings. Sprinkle with lemon juice, salt, and pepper. Bake in moderate 325° oven about 45 minutes or until done. Make flake test beside bone.

Planked Fish   Rub plank with oil and heat in moderate 375° oven 10 minutes. Prepare as indicated for Baked Split Whole or Fillets and Steaks. Bake in moderate 350° oven allowing about 15 minutes to the pound, or broil in preheated broiler 20 minutes—make flake test for doneness.

Surround with Duchess potatoes (mashed with beaten egg). Brush potatoes with melted butter or milk or egg yolk. Brown under broiler. Add other vegetables if desired.

Boiled and Steamed Fish   Wrap fish in a piece of cheesecloth. Simmer very gently in water to cover. Season with ½ tsp. salt, ½ tbsp. lemon juice or vinegar. Cover. Simmer fillets about 8 minutes, whole fish about 15 minutes according to thickness. Test as for baked fish. Fish should not be pink near bones. To steam: Season and place in steamer or colander over boiling water. Cover. Allow 6–15 minutes according to thickness. Test with fork. Good cold, creamed, or as is.

Poached Fish   Same as for boiled. To poach: use greased, deep frying pan, cover with equal parts milk and water or dry white wine and water. Simmer tightly covered, about 5–10 minutes per pound. Test as for baked fish. Use liquid as base for sauce. Good cold, creamed, or as is.

Sautéed (Pan-fried) Fish   Remove heads, tails from tiny whole fish; cut larger ones into serving pieces. Dry well. Dip in beaten egg, roll in seasoned crumbs, flour, or corn meal. Melt fat or oil about ½ inch deep in heavy skillet. If not skinned, place skin side down. Brown slowly 4–5 minutes. Turn once with spatula. Cook until fish flakes when tried with fork. Drain on absorbent paper.

Deep-fried Fish   Prepare as above. It's a good idea to dip in egg and crumb mixture twice. Arrange only one layer in frying basket. Immerse in deep fat or oil heated to 375° or hot enough to brown a bread cube in 60 seconds. Fry until nicely browned. Drain on absorbent paper.

Broiled Fish   Sprinkle fish with salt and pepper. Brush nonfatty fish with melted butter, oil, or bacon drippings. Place split fish or thick steaks on greased broiler rack, skin side up; fillets and thin steaks on greased pan. Cook in preheated broiler 3 inches below heat. Turn once. Do not turn thin fillets. Allow about 20–30 minutes for whole,

15–20 for split fish, 10–15 minutes for 1–1½-inch-thick steaks. Test as for baked fish. Brush frequently with melted butter or oil.

Frozen Fish Keep frozen packages in freezer tray until needed. If less than the whole package is needed, divide it by chopping with ice pick. Keep the rest rewrapped and solidly frozen until required. In some instances defrosting is unnecessary. However, pieces frozen together that require coating or are to be cooked separately must be at least partially defrosted. Defrost slowly in refrigerator or at room temperature. Cook as soon as defrosted and still cold. Never cook hard-frozen fish at high heat—the outside scorches before the inside is cooked. Use the same cooking methods as for fresh fish.

Leftover Fish

ANNA'S FISH AND CHIPS

Leftover
COOKED FISH, flaked, at least 1 cup
or
TUNA, 1 7-ounce can
and

Cream cheese, 2 packages	Worcestershire sauce, ½ tsp.
Mayonnaise, 1 tbsp.	
Sherry, ¼ cup	Minced onion, ½ tsp.
Capers, 2 tbsp.	Garlic salt, ¼ tsp.
Chopped parsley, 2 tbsp.	Potato chips, 2 cups

In top of double boiler, blend cheese with mayonnaise and sherry until smooth. Add fish, capers, parsley, Worcestershire, onion, and garlic salt. Heat over boiling water a few minutes. Do not boil. Serve surrounded by potato chips. SERVES 2–3.

Variation: Mix all the ingredients. Do not heat. Chill in refrigerator. Garnish with paprika. Serve as appetizer on potato chips or with crackers.

Suggested: Serve with torn iceberg lettuce and green

pepper salad, Mustard Dressing[R]—and buttered pumper-nickel slices.

CURRIED RICE AND FISH FLAKE SALAD

Leftover
   COOKED FISH[S], at least 1½ cups, boned and flaked
and

Cooked rice, 2½ cups	Lemon juice, 1 tbsp.
French dressing (2 tbsp. salad oil and 1 tbsp. vinegar)	Curry powder, 1½ tsp.
	Peas (optional), ½ cup
	Chopped celery, ½ cup
Parsley, ⅓ cup	Chutney, ½ tbsp.
Mayonnaise, ½ cup	

Substitute: Cooked chicken cut into small dice, or flaked, canned tuna.

Chill rice in French dressing with 2 tbsp. parsley. Blend mayonnaise with lemon juice, curry powder, and rest of parsley. Add fish, peas, and celery. Chill. Just before serving, place rice on serving platter; top with fish mixture; garnish with chutney. THIS IS AN APPETIZER OR SIDE DISH FOR 4—AS A MAIN COURSE SERVES 2.

Suggested: As a main course, serve with hot buttermilk biscuits and a variety of cheeses.

FAVORITE FISH SALAD

Leftover
   COOKED FISH, boned, at least 1½ cups
and

Mayonnaise, ¼ cup	Diced celery, 2 tbsp.
French dressing, ¼ cup	Diced, peeled avocado, 1
Paper-thin onion rings, ¼ cup	Salt and pepper to taste
	Mixed salad greens
Diced, pared cucumber, ½ cup	Chopped hard-cooked eggs, 2
Chopped tomato, ½ cup	

Combine mayonnaise, French dressing, onion rings, cucumber, tomato, celery, avocado, salt, pepper, and fish. Chill well. Serve on mixed greens. Garnish with eggs. Wonderful with hot buttermilk biscuits. THIS IS A MAIN COURSE FOR 2–3.

Suggested: Serve with individual bowls of German Bread Soup[R].

FISH FRITTERS

Leftover
COOKED FISH, at least 1½ cups
and

Well-beaten egg yolks, 3	Minced parsley, 1 tbsp.
Flour, 3 tbsp.	Stiffly beaten egg whites, 3
Salt and pepper to taste	Deep fat
Onion juice, 1 tbsp.	

Free fish of skin and bones. Mash well. Blend with egg yolks, flour, salt, pepper, onion juice, and parsley. Fold in egg whites. Drop by spoonfuls in hot fat (375°–385°) and fry until golden. Drain. SERVES 3–4.

Suggested: Serve with Corn Kernel Pie[R], sliced cucumber and relishes salad—plus poppy-seed rolls.

FISH 'N CHEESE CASSEROLE

Leftover
   COOKED FISH, flaked and boned, at least 1½ cups
and

Milk, 1 cup	Chopped parsley, 1 tbsp.
Butter or margarine, 1½ tbsp.	Minced onion, 1½ tbsp.
	Salt and pepper to taste
Bread crumbs, ¾ cup	Well-beaten eggs, 2
Grated Cheddar cheese, 1 cup	Diced boiled potatoes, 1–1½ cups
Chopped pimento, 3 tbsp.	

Warm milk, add butter, stir until melted. Pour into bowl. Stir in bread crumbs, cheese, pimento, parsley, onion, salt, and pepper; mix well. Stir in eggs. Arrange fish and potatoes on bottom of buttered casserole. Pour cheese mixture over all. Place casserole in pan of water. Bake in moderate 325° (preheated) oven about 1 hour. SERVES 3–4.

Suggested: Serve with buttered Frenched green beans, tossed salad with Russian Dressing[R]—and Parker House rolls.

FRENCH FISH PUFF

Leftover
   COOKED FISH, boned and mashed to paste, at least 1½ cups
and

Salt and pepper to taste	
Onion juice, 1 tbsp.	Grated American Cheese, 1½ cups
Tabasco (optional), 2 drops	Slightly beaten eggs, 2
Minced parsley, 1 tsp.	Milk, 1 cup
Buttered bread, cut into cubes, 6 slices	Sherry, ⅓ cup
	Worcestershire sauce, dash

Mash fish with salt, pepper, onion juice, Tabasco, and parsley. Arrange bread cubes, cheese, and fish in alternate layers in shallow buttered baking dish. Top with layer of bread cubes. Mix eggs, milk, sherry, and Worcestershire. Season to taste. Pour over mixture in baking dish. Bake in moderate 325° oven 1 hour. SERVES 3–4.

Suggested: Serve with Ever-Welcome Potato Salad[R].

GLOUCESTER SNACK

Leftover
COOKED FISH, boned and chopped, at least 2 cups
and

Butter or margarine, 2 tbsp.	Chopped green pepper, 1 tbsp.
Cream of celery soup, 1 can	Worcestershire sauce, 1 tsp.
Milk, ⅓ cup	Rusks or toasted rye bread

Melt butter in chafing dish. Add fish and soup, milk, and green pepper. Heat slowly and thoroughly. Remove from heat and add Worcestershire. Serve at once on rusks or toasted rye bread. SERVES 3–4.

Suggested: Serve with baked potatoes and cabbage slaw.

ISLAND LOAF

Leftover
COOKED HALIBUT⁸, flaked, at least 1 cup
and

Melted butter or margarine, 3 tbsp.	Soft bread crumbs, ¼ cup
Worcestershire sauce, 1 tbsp.	Milk and/or fish stock, ¼ cup
Slightly beaten egg, 1	Cooked rice, 2½ cups
Salt and pepper to taste	Sliced hard-cooked egg, 1
	Butter, 2 tbsp.

Substitute: Chicken, salmon, or tuna.

Combine fish with butter, Worcestershire, egg, salt, pepper, bread crumbs, and milk. Line buttered loaf pan with 2 cups rice. Add fish mixture. Top with layer of sliced egg. Cover with remaining rice. Dot generously with butter. Place in shallow pan of hot water. Bake in moderate 350° oven 40 minutes. SERVES 2–3.

Suggested: Serve with buttered peas and carrots, olives, celery, and relishes—plus hot cross buns.

INDIAN KEDGEREE

Leftover
COOKED FISH, boned and flaked, at least 1½ cups
and

Butter or margarine, ½ cup (¼ pound)	Salt, 1 tsp.
Cooked rice, 2½ cups	Pepper, ¼ tsp.
Chopped hard-boiled eggs, 2–3	Curry powder (optional), ½ tsp.

Melt butter until bubbling. Mix in fish, rice, eggs, salt, pepper, and curry powder. Stir with wooden fork, to keep from sticking to pan. Cook slowly until thoroughly heated. SERVES 3–4.

Suggested: Serve with Almond Spinach Croquettes[R], head lettuce with Roquefort Dressing[R]—and rye bread.

FISH PUFF SPECIALE

Leftover
COOKED FISH, 1½ cups boned and coarsely chopped *and*

Butter, 6 tbsp.	Salt and pepper to taste
Chopped celery, 2 stalks	Milk, ½ cup
Chopped onion, 1 medium	Rich chicken broth, ¼
Chopped carrot, 1	cup
Cognac, 2 tbsp.	Beaten egg yolks, 3
White wine, ¼ cup	Stiffly beaten egg whites,
Cream, ½ cup	4–5
Flour, 2½ tbsp.	

Melt 3 tbsp. butter in saucepan. Cook celery, onion, and carrot until onion is soft. Add fish and cognac. Heat. Set aflame. Add the wine and simmer uncovered until wine is halved. Add cream. Heat. Pour into buttered soufflé dish. Melt remaining butter. Stir in flour, salt, and pepper. Gradually add milk and chicken broth. Stir until thick and smooth. Remove from heat. Stir in egg yolks. Fold in egg whites. Pour over fish mixture. Place in hot 425° oven for 20 minutes or until golden brown and puffy. SERVES 3–4.

Suggested: Serve with Quick 'n Easy Potatoes[R]—and buttered rye toast slices.

MONSEIGNEUR EGGS

Leftover
  COOKED FISH, boned and finely chopped, at least 1½
  cups
and

Piecrust mix, ½ package	Worcestershire sauce to
Butter or margarine, 1	taste
tbsp.	Well-beaten eggs, 3
Flour, 1 tbsp.	Finely chopped hard-
Salt, ½ tsp.	boiled egg, 1
Milk, ½ cup	Butter, 1 tbsp.
Salt and pepper to taste	

Prepare and bake 8-inch pie shell as directed on package.
Melt butter in saucepan. Blend in flour and salt. Add
milk. Stir until thick and smooth. Do not boil. Add fish.
Season with salt, pepper, and Worcestershire; stir in eggs.
Pour into baked pastry shell. Top with chopped egg
and dot with butter. Bake in moderate 350° oven until
set, about 15 minutes. SERVES 3–4.

Suggested: Serve with Green Bean Salad Bowl[R], pilot
crackers—and mixed cheeses.

PAWTUCKET FISH

Leftover
  COOKED FISH[S], flaked and boned, at least 1½ cups
and

Butter or margarine, 2	Worcestershire sauce, 1
tbsp.	tsp.
Flour, 3 tbsp.	Well-beaten egg yolk, 1
Milk plus fish liquid, 1½	Grated cheese, ¼ cup
cups	Buttered bread crumbs,
Salt, ½ tsp.	¼ cup

Substitute: Canned crab meat, tuna, or salmon.

Melt butter in saucepan. Blend in flour; add milk and fish liquid. Simmer, stirring, until thick and smooth. Add salt and Worcestershire; remove from heat. Stir in egg yolk; fold in fish flakes. Fill 4 individual buttered baking dishes or 1 shallow one. Sprinkle with grated cheese. Top with buttered crumbs. Bake in moderate 375° oven about 20 minutes until top is brown. SERVES 3–4.

Suggested: Serve with Cheese, Tomatoes, and Lima Beans[R]—plus poppy-seed rolls.

POSITANESE FISH SOUP

Leftover
    BOILED or STEAMED or BROILED FISH, at least 1 cup, plus fish liquid or pan drippings
and

Oil, 3 tbsp.	Saffron, ¼ tsp.
Chopped onions, 2 small	Bay leaf, 1
Sliced leek, 1	Chopped parsley, 1 tbsp.
Minced garlic clove, 1	Chopped tomatoes, 3
Tiny red pepper pod	Diced potatoes, 3 large
(optional), 1	Water, 1½ cups
Salt and pepper to taste	Garlic-rubbed toast

Heat oil. Add onions, leek, garlic, and red pepper. Cook until onions soften. Add salt, pepper, saffron, bay leaf, parsley, and tomatoes. Bring to boil; simmer 5 minutes. Add potatoes, fish liquid and/or drippings, if any, and water. Simmer until potatoes are tender—about 20 minutes. Remove red pepper. Add boned and flaked fish. Bring to boil. Serve with garlic-rubbed toast. SERVES 2–3.

SALEM FISH 'N CHUTNEY TARTS

Leftover
  COOKED FISH, 1 cup, boned and flaked
or
  TUNA, 1 7-ounce can
and

Piecrust mix	Finely chopped onion, 1
Chopped chutney, ¼ cup	tbsp.
Finely chopped green	Mayonnaise, ⅓ cup
pepper, 1 tbsp.	Beaten egg, 1

Prepare dough as directed on package. Roll to 12 × 12 inches, about ⅛ inch thick. Cut into 4 squares. Mix chutney, green pepper, onion, and mayonnaise with flaked fish. Put a heaping of mixture in center of each square. Bring all points of dough to center. Pinch seams together with wet fingers or seal with beaten egg. Brush tops with beaten egg. Bake in hot 425° oven about 10 minutes —until golden brown. MAKES 4 SERVINGS.

Suggested: Bake an all-in-the-oven meal. Serve with broccoli—and hot baked potatoes.

CLAM AND CORN CASSEROLE

Leftover
  CLAMS, at least 1 cup minced, or 1 8-ounce can with liquid
and

Butter or margarine, 2	Pimento (optional), 1
tbsp.	tbsp.
Flour, 2 tbsp.	Onion, 2 tbsp.
Milk plus clam liquid,	Finely chopped parsley, 1
¾ cup	tbsp.
Eggs, 1 whole, 1 yolk	Dry mustard, ½ tsp.
Corn, 1 cup—or 1 8-oz. can	Salt, ½ tsp.
	Lemon juice, 1 tsp.

Melt butter in saucepan. Blend in flour. Add milk and clam liquid. Simmer, stirring, until thick and smooth. Beat eggs, add clams, corn, pimento, onion, parsley, mustard, salt, and lemon juice. Stir in white sauce. Turn into buttered casserole. Bake in moderate 350° oven 45 minutes. SERVES 2.

Suggested: Serve with potato chips, Asparagus and Olive Salad[R]—and hot buttered biscuits.

CLAM CHOWDER

Leftover
  CLAMS, minced, at least 1 cup
and

Diced salt pork or bacon, 3 tbsp.	Water and/or clam liquid, ½ cup
Chopped onion, 3 tbsp.	Milk, 3 cups
Thinly sliced potatoes, 1½ cups	Butter or margarine, 1 tbsp.
Salt, ¾ tsp.	Paprika
Pepper, ¼ tsp.	

Cook salt pork or bacon in kettle until golden brown. Add onion and stir frequently until onion is tender but not brown. Add potatoes, salt, pepper, and water and/or clam liquid. Simmer covered until potatoes are tender, about 15 minutes. Add clams and milk; bring to boiling point. Just before serving, add butter. Serve garnished with paprika. SERVES 4.

Suggested: Serve with macaroni and cheese, iceberg lettuce, chopped scallions, and grated carrot salad and Horseradish Dressing[R].

SEAFOOD TOSSED SALAD

Leftover
   COOKED SHRIMP or LOBSTER or CRAB MEAT, shelled
   and diced, at least ¾ cup
and

Salad oil, 4 tbsp.	Sour cream, ¼ cup
Lemon juice, 1½ tbsp.	Sliced pimento-stuffed
Salt, 1 tsp.	olives, ½ cup
Pepper to taste	Chopped tomato, 1
Grated onion, ½ tsp.	medium
Dry mustard, pinch	Shredded lettuce, 3 cups

Combine oil, lemon juice, salt, and pepper with onion,
mustard, and sour cream. Beat well. Place fish (if using
shrimp, devein), olives, tomato, and lettuce in salad
bowl. Toss with dressing. THIS IS AN APPETIZER OR AC-
COMPANYING SALAD—SERVES 4.

Suggested: Serve with Broccoli Soufflé Gourmet[R]—plus
toasted English muffins.

SHRIMPS AMEN

Leftover
   COOKED SHRIMP, shelled and deveined, at least 1½
   cups
and

Salad oil, ¼ cup	Minced green pepper, 1
Lemon juice, 1½ tbsp.	tbsp.
Salt, 1 tsp.	Diced tomato, 1
Pepper to taste	Sliced stuffed olives, ½
Dry mustard, ⅛ tsp.	cup
Curry powder, 1 tsp.	Coarsely chunked lettuce
Minced pearl onion, 1	
small	

Beat salad oil with lemon juice, salt, pepper, mustard,
curry powder, onion, and green pepper. Toss with to-

mato, olives, shrimp. Chill well. Toss with lettuce. SERVES 4 AS AN APPETIZER OR ACCOMPANYING SALAD.

Variation: If you have any leftover cooked rice, toss it in too.

Suggested: Serve as an appetizer followed by Florentine Ramekin Eggs[R]—plus hot French bread.

CAROLINA SHRIMP AND CUCUMBER

Leftover
COOKED SHRIMP, shelled and deveined, at least ¾ cup
and

Fat, 2 tbsp.	Salt to taste
Sliced onion, 1	Paprika, ⅛ tsp.
Flour, 2 tbsp.	Cooked rice, 2 cups
Milk, 1 cup	Crushed corn flakes, ¼ cup
Peeled and chopped, parboiled cucumber[S], 1 cup	Butter, 1 tbsp.

Substitute: Boiled eggplant or green beans.

Brown onion in fat. Blend in flour, stir in milk. Simmer, stirring constantly until thick and smooth. Add cucumber, shrimp, salt, paprika, and rice. Heat thoroughly. Turn into oven-proof serving dish, sprinkle with corn flakes, dot with butter. Brown quickly under broiler. SERVES 2–3.

Suggested: Serve with Quick 'n Easys Beets and Celery[R] —and hot corn pones.

SHRIMP CREOLE

Leftover
COOKED SHRIMP, shelled and deveined, at least 1 cup
and

Fat, 1 tbsp.	Tomatoes, 1 No. 1 can
Chopped celery, ¼ cup	Vinegar, 1 tsp.
Sliced onion, 1	Chili powder, 1 tsp. or
Flour, 1 tbsp.	more to taste
Sugar, pinch	Cooked or frozen peas, 1
Salt, ½ tsp.	cup
Water, pea liquid and/or	
bouillon, ¾ cup	

Sauté celery and onion in fat until brown. Blend in flour, sugar, and salt. Add liquids. Simmer, stirring, until thick and smooth. Add tomatoes, vinegar, and chili powder. Simmer very slowly 25 minutes. Add shrimp and peas. Cook another 5 minutes. (If frozen peas are used, cook until tender—about 7 minutes.) SERVES 2–3.

Suggested: Serve on split baked potatoes plus Chinese cabbage tossed salad with Sour Cream Dressing[R]—piping hot toast triangles.

CHICOPEE

Leftover
COOKED LOBSTER MEAT[S], at least ¾ cup, shelled and diced
and

Hard-cooked eggs, 2	Salt and pepper to taste
Butter or margarine, 1	Paprika, few grains
tbsp.	Chopped parsley, 1 tbsp.
Flour, 1 tbsp.	Worcestershire sauce, 1
Milk, 1¼ cups	tbsp.

Substitute: Shrimp, deveined, or crab meat.

Shell eggs, separate whites from yolks. Mash yolks. Melt butter in saucepan. Blend in flour. Add yolks. Stir in milk. Keep stirring until thick and smooth. Add lobster meat, chopped egg whites, salt, pepper, paprika, parsley, and Worcestershire. Cook slowly 10 minutes. Pour into patty shells or serve over toast. SERVES 2–3.

Suggested: Serve with Vegetable Puffs[R], tomato and watercress salad—and hot buttered rolls.

COQUILLE ST. JACQUES

Leftover
  BOILED SCALLOPS, cut up, at least 1½ cups
and

Butter or margarine, 3 tbsp.

Chopped onion, 2 tbsp.

Flour, 3 tbsp.

Prepared mustard, ½ tsp.

Salt, ½ tsp.

Cayenne, few specks

Milk, 1¼ cups

White wine, 2 tbsp.

Worcestershire sauce, 1 tsp.

Grated Parmesan, ¼ cup plus 2 tbsp.

Chopped, cooked or canned shrimp—or other cooked shellfish—½ cup

Chopped parsley, 1 tbsp.

Brown onion in butter. Blend in flour. Add mustard, salt, and cayenne. Add milk and wine, stirring constantly until thick and smooth; remove from heat. Add Worcestershire, ¼ cup grated cheese, scallops, shellfish, and parsley. Turn into 4 large scallop shells or ramekins. Top with remaining grated cheese. Place under broiler until piping hot and nicely browned. MAKES 4 SERVINGS.

Suggested: Serve with French fried potatoes, Mixed Beet Ring Mold[R]—and clover leaf rolls.

POULTRY

POULTRY

Poultry perhaps more than any other food has been most adapted to our needs. Gone are the days of the seasonal chicken, spring broilers, summer fryers, fall roasters. You can buy poultry fresh, frozen, dressed, undressed, all white meat, small turkeys, drumsticks only, bred with or without wings, more or less breast—and who knows what will come next. This means we have almost unlimited choice for variety, imagination, and tasty nourishment.

It is easy to buy poultry. Check labels, tags, and stamps for quality, weight, style, and price. Note government grades and processor's brand.

Buy with planned leftovers in mind. Remember that the price per pound for a ready-to-cook bird is more than the same quality for "dressed" one—but count on 25–30 per cent waste since a dressed bird has head, feet, and entrails. Store cooked birds covered in refrigerator, stuffing removed. Use within 4 to 5 days. It's a good idea to remove meat from bones, too. You can make a broth from these. Do not keep birds in the water they've been cooked in. Remove and store broth separately.

Poultry is a real challenge. Its variations are unlimited. The following leftovers, as always, are wonderfully flexible and proportions may vary with what you have on hand. More or less poultry or vegetables may be used. Frozen, fresh, or canned foods may be substituted. Adjust cooking time accordingly. See sauce section for still more variations.

Basic Cooking Instructions for Poultry

Stuffing and Trussing Stuffing may be prepared in advance, but do not stuff until roasting time. Allow 1–1¼ cups stuffing per ready-to-cook pound. Rub body cavity with salt. Spoon in stuffing. Pack loosely. Fasten neck skin onto back with pins or toothpicks. Sew or close cavity with poultry pins or skewers. Skewer wings against side or twist against the back so they lie flat and tie closely together. Press legs together at tip ends, tying down around tail so they are held against body.

Roasting For chicken, roast in slow 300° oven, 30–45 minutes per pound; for turkey (8–10 pounds), duck, capon allow 20–30 minutes per pound at 325°. Place on rack, breast side up, uncovered. Rub skin all over with butter, margarine, oil, or melted fat or cover with strips of bacon or salt pork. Add no water. Baste a few times, do not turn. (Or, if you've a V-shaped rack, roast breast side down and turn for the second half of the cooking.) If using a thermometer, insert into thigh near body. Roast until the thermometer reads 190° or until drumstick moves easily and meat feels very soft around thickest part of drumstick. Insert fork or knife; juice should be colorless. (Ducks are very fatty; do not add more fat. Prick skin with fork to allow fat to run out. Do not baste. Pour off excess fat during roasting.) Remove toothpicks, string, or skewers before serving.

Pan Frying Chickens for frying may be prepared two ways: (1) Wash pieces and dust, without drying, in seasoned flour or corn meal mixed with flour *or* (2) Dip pieces in fine cracker or bread crumbs, flour, or corn meal, then in beaten egg mixed with 2 tbsp. milk or water, and again in the crumbs, etc. Heat oil or fat in skillet to a depth of about ½ inch. Place pieces in hot fat and brown on all sides. Reduce heat and cook until tender, about 30–40 minutes, covered or uncovered.

Deep Frying Small broilers may be disjointed and deep fried. Follow method No. 2 above or dip pieces in this batter: Stir 1 cup flour into 1 beaten egg mixed with ¾ cup milk. Add 1 tsp. salt and ⅛ tsp. pepper. Stir in 1 tsp. melted butter. Heat fat or oil to 375° or until hot enough to brown a bread cube in about 60 seconds. Lower in only a few pieces at a time. Fry about 15–20 minutes until tender.

Broiling Large birds should be cut in quarters, smaller ones in halves lengthwise; neck and backbone removed. Snap and break cartilage at joints, do not cut. Brush with melted butter, fat, or oil. Sprinkle with salt and pepper. Broil skin side down in broiler (preheated or not, according to manufacturer's directions) about 4–5 inches from heat. Broil under medium heat until brown, about 10 minutes. Turn and brush. After 15 minutes turn again. Keep turning and brushing every 10 minutes until done (25–40 minutes). To test for doneness insert fork or knife into drumstick. Juice should be colorless, meat not pink.

Frozen Poultry Frozen chickens may be roasted without thawing. Remove giblets from cavity, allow approximately double the cooking period indicated above. Or defrost slowly in refrigerator to prevent shrinkage and loss of juice, allowing 3–6 hours per pound. Or defrost at room temperature allowing 1 hour per pound. Cook birds as soon as defrosted and still cold. Disjointed birds should be completely defrosted before frying. Never defrost even a stewing chicken under running water.

Leftover Poultry

QUICK 'N EASYS

Leftover
   HAM or CHICKEN or TURKEY or WHAT-HAVE-YOU MEATS, cut into bite sizes

Make a sauce using any one of the condensed creamed soups—mushroom, celery, potato, chicken, asparagus, pea, etc. Dilute with ⅓ cup milk—or refer to sauce section. Add the leftover and some diced pimento. Serve on quick-cooking rice.

Variations:
    Add ¼ cup blanched, then sautéed, chopped almonds.
    Add ½ cup chopped parsley.
    Serve in scooped out avocados.
    Add chopped celery.
    Add chopped hard-cooked eggs.
    Place in buttered casserole, top with biscuit dough, and bake in oven until dough is done.

Soup Garnish: Almost any poultry, cut in julienne style—that is, in thin matchstick strips, may be used as a soup garnish.

ASPARAGUS HOLLANDA

Leftover
    COOKED CHICKEN or TURKEY[s], chopped, at least 1 cup
and

Quick-frozen or cooked asparagus, 1 box	Butter or margarine, 6 tbsp.
Quick-frozen or cooked peas, 1½ cups	Flour, 2 tbsp.
Bread, 8 half slices	Milk, 1 cup
Well-beaten egg, 1, mixed with ½ cup milk	Lemon juice, 1 tbsp.
	Salt and pepper to taste
	Pimento slivers

Substitute: Cooked or canned crab meat.

If frozen, prepare asparagus and peas as directed on box; keep hot. Dip bread into egg-milk mixture. Sauté in 3 tbsp. butter until golden on both sides. Keep warm. Heat 3 tbsp. butter, blend in flour; stir in milk, stirring until smooth and thickened. Add chicken, lemon juice, salt, and pepper. Heat. Arrange hot asparagus on French toast. Circle with hot peas and pour creamed chicken over all. Garnish with pimento. SERVES 3–4.

Suggested: Serve with tossed greens salad, French Dressing[R]—and assorted cheese tray.

BARCELONA LOAF

Leftover
COOKED or CANNED CHICKEN, cut into small pieces, at least 1 cup
and

Cooked rice, 1 cup	Paprika, ¼ tsp.
Slightly beaten egg, 1	Diced pimento, 2 tsp.
Bread crumbs, ¼ cup	Minced onion, 1 tsp.
Tomato juice, ⅓ cup	Diced celery, ¼ cup
Salt, ¼ tsp.	Diced green pepper, ¼ cup

Blend rice, egg, bread crumbs, tomato juice, salt, paprika, pimento, onion, celery, and green pepper with chicken. Pour into small well-greased loaf pan. Bake in moderate 375° oven until firm—about 35 minutes. Loosen from sides and unmold on serving dish. SERVES 2–3.

Suggested: Serve with sliced tomatoes, paper-thin onion rings, French Dressing[R]—and soft rolls.

CHICKEN AND ALMOND MOUSSE

Leftover
COOKED or CANNED CHICKEN, finely diced, boned, at least 1 cup
and

Unflavored gelatin, 1 envelope, plus ¼ cup water	Chopped blanched almonds, ¼ cup
Chicken broth or cube dissolved in water, 1½ cups	Chutney, 1½ tbsp.
	Mayonnaise, ½ cup
Cooked peas, 1 cup	Avocado or pineapple
	Lettuce leaves, 4

Soften gelatin in cold water 5 minutes. Add to broth, stir until dissolved. Cool until slightly thickened. Add chicken, peas, almonds, chutney, and mayonnaise; mix well. Pour into ring mold. Chill until set. Serve with sliced avocado or pineapple chunks on perfect crisp lettuce leaves. SERVES 2–3.

Suggested: Serve with buttered corn on the cob—and toasted rolls.

CHICKEN BRUNSWICK

Leftover
  COOKED CHICKEN, at least 1 cup cut in dice, or 1 7-ounce can
and

Condensed mushroom or celery soup	Chopped hard-boiled eggs, 2
White wine, ¼ cup	Salt and pepper to taste
Crushed corn flakes or potato chips, ½ cup plus 2 tbsp.	

Blend soup and wine together. Add chicken, ½ cup corn flakes or potato-chip crumbs, eggs, salt, and pepper; mix well. Turn into shallow buttered casserole. Sprinkle with remaining 2 tbsp. corn flakes or potato-chip crumbs. Bake in moderate 375° oven 20 minutes. SERVES 2–3.

Suggested: Serve with Corn Chowder[R]—and hot buttered popovers.

CHICKEN CORN MEAL

Leftover
  COOKED or CANNED CHICKEN[S], finely diced, at
  least 1 cup
and

Corn meal, 1 cup	basil, 1 tbsp. chopped
Boiling water, 4 cups	celery, salt and pepper
Salt, 1½ tsp.	to taste
Gravy, at least 1 cup OR 3	Grated cheese, ¼ cup
finely diced tomatoes,	Butter or margarine, 1
½ cup water, ½ tsp.	tbsp.

Substitute (or mix with): Cooked or canned diced ham.

Make a corn-meal mush by stirring corn meal slowly into
boiling salted water. Cook and stir over low heat until
thick. Reheat chicken and gravy—OR heat tomatoes with
½ cup water, basil, celery, salt, and pepper. Simmer covered ½ hour. Add chicken. Cook another 5 minutes. Line
shallow pan with half the corn-meal mush. Pour chicken
and sauce (or hot gravy), less 2 tbsp., over mush. Add
rest of mush. Cover with remaining sauce. Sprinkle with
cheese, dot with butter; brown quickly in hot 425° oven
10 minutes. SERVES 2–3.

Suggested: Serve with sliced cucumbers in Sour Cream
Dressing[R]—and rye bread.

CHICKEN LEMON MADRILÈNE

Leftover
  COOKED CHICKEN, at least 1 cup
and

Consommé Madrilène, 2	Whole cloves, 2
cans	Paper-thin lemon slices, 8

Heat soup with whole cloves. Add chicken; bring to boil.
Add half the lemon slices; simmer very slowly 5 minutes.

Discard lemon. Serve immediately—add fresh lemon slices just before serving. Overcooking makes soup bitter. SERVES 4.

Suggested: Serve with Ham and Scalloped Sweets[R], mixed Boston lettuce and chicory salad with Cucumber Dressing[R]—and rye bread.

CHICKEN MEXICAINE

Leftover
COOKED CHICKEN, at least 2 cups, cut in large pieces
and

Butter or margarine, 1 tbsp.	Tomatoes, 8-ounce can
Finely chopped onion, ¼ cup	Button mushrooms, 1 4-ounce can
Finely chopped green pepper, 1	Chopped parsley, 2 tbsp.
Minced garlic clove, 1	Sugar, ½ tsp.
Flour, 2 tbsp.	Fresh ground black pepper to taste
Chicken broth or 2 cubes and water to make 1 cup	Chili powder, 1 tsp. or more
	Orégano, ¼ tsp.
	Salt to taste

Melt butter in skillet. Add onion, green pepper, and garlic; cook until onion is soft. Blend in flour. Add chicken broth, tomatoes, mushrooms, parsley, sugar, black pepper, chili powder, orégano, and salt, stirring until slightly thick and smooth. Place chicken in shallow casserole. Pour sauce over. Bake in medium hot 400° oven 30 minutes. SERVES 3–4.

Suggested: Serve on hot corn bread—plus a salad of sliced green peppers, diced cucumbers, and lettuce with garlic French Dressing[R].

CHICKEN PAPRIKA

Leftover
COOKED CHICKEN, at least 4 slices, or 1½ cups
and

Fat, 2 tbsp.	Egg yolk, 1 beaten with 1
Sliced onion, 1 large	cup sour cream
Paprika, 1 tbsp.	Salt and pepper to taste

Sauté onion in hot fat until golden brown. Add chicken and paprika. Cook 5 minutes. Add egg yolk-sour cream mixture, salt, and pepper. Simmer very slowly 10 minutes. SERVES 3-4.

Suggested: Serve on buttered noodles with Mushroom Croquettes[R]—and buttered rye bread slices.

CHICKEN YORKSHIRE

Leftover
COOKED or CANNED CHICKEN, at least 2 cups, diced
and

Melted butter or	combined with 2 tbsp.
margarine, 2 tbsp.	chicken drippings and 1
Flour, 1 cup	cup milk
Baking powder, ¼ tsp.	Leftover gravy, 1 cup—or
Salt, ½ tsp.	canned cream of
Well-beaten eggs, 2,	chicken soup

Place chicken in greased baking dish; brush with butter. Sift flour, baking powder, and salt together. Gradually stir in combined eggs, drippings, and milk. Beat until smooth and free of lumps. The batter should be quite thin. Pour over chicken. Bake in moderate 350° oven 25-30 minutes. Serve from baking dish with gravy or cream of chicken soup. SERVES 3-4.

Suggested: Serve with buttered asparagus, mustard greens, and Boston lettuce salad—plus bread sticks.

CORN-PONE MOLD

Leftover
COOKED CHICKEN or TURKEY, cut into strips, at least
1½ cups
and

Cream-style corn, 1 No. 1 picnic can
Tomato juice, ¾ cup
Grated American cheese, ½ cup
Salt, ½ tsp.
Pepper to taste
Tabasco, 3 drops
Chopped onion, ¼ cup
Minced green pepper, 2 tbsp.
Corn meal, ½ cup
Well-beaten eggs, 2
Milk, ¾ cup
Condensed cream of chicken soup, 1 can
Chopped pimento, 2 tbsp.
Grated American cheese, 2 tbsp.

Mix creamed corn with tomato juice, cheese, salt, pepper, Tabasco, onion, green pepper, and corn meal; add eggs and ½ cup milk. Pour into well-buttered ring mold. Place in pan of hot water. Bake in slow 300° oven until firm—about 1 hour. Loosen edges with spatula. Meanwhile, mix chicken soup with remaining milk. Heat. Add chicken and pimento. To serve: Reverse corn-pone mold onto oven-proof platter. Fill center and top with chicken sauce. Top with 2 tbsp. grated cheese. Brown quickly under broiler. SERVES 4–5.

Suggested: Serve with buttered hot beets and tomato-endive salad with French Dressing[R].

CREAMED CHICKEN CANTONESE

Leftover
COOKED or CANNED CHICKEN, diced, at least 1½ cups
and

Cream of mushroom soup, 1 can	Sliced water chestnuts, 1 can, drained
Sliced mushrooms, 1 4-ounce can, plus liquid	Marjoram, pinch
Milk, 1½ cups	Cornstarch, 3 tbsp.
Sautéed chopped almonds, ¼ cup	Milk, 2 tbsp.
	Soy sauce, 2 tbsp.
	Salt and pepper to taste
	Boiled noodles[s], ½ pound

Substitute: Canned Chinese fried noodles.

Heat mushroom soup in saucepan with mushrooms and liquid, milk, almonds, water chestnuts, marjoram, and chicken. Blend cornstarch with 2 tbsp. cold milk and soy sauce. Add to sauce. Add salt and pepper to taste. Simmer slowly for 10 minutes. Stir in drained noodles. Cook 1 minute more. SERVES 3–4.

Suggested: Serve with orange, onion rings, and endive salad marinated in French Dressing[R]—and toast triangles.

CREOLE CHICKEN

Leftover
COOKED CHICKEN, at least 1 cup or 1 7-ounce can, diced
and

Chicken fat or bacon drippings, 2 tbsp.

Uncooked white rice, 1 cup

Chopped green pepper, 2 tbsp.

Chopped onion, 1

Tomatoes, 5, cut into strips —or No. 2 can (and only one cup water)

Water, 2 cups

Salt, 1 tsp.

Sage, ¼ tsp.

Condensed cream of chicken soup, 1 can—or 1 cup white sauce plus 1 chicken cube dissolved in 2 tbsp. boiling water

Milk, ¾ cup

Melt chicken fat or bacon drippings in skillet. Add rice, green pepper, and onion. Stir until browned (about 5 minutes). Add tomatoes, water, salt, and sage. Cover tightly. Cook over very low heat 20 minutes or until rice is tender. Meanwhile, combine chicken, soup, and milk in saucepan. Stir until smooth and heat thoroughly. Heap rice on serving platter. Make a deep well in center and fill with the chicken. SERVES 3–4.

Variation: Add 1 can drained okra to chicken mixture.

Suggested: Serve with Lima Bean Bacon Pot[R], tossed Boston lettuce salad with lemon French Dressing[R]—and buttermilk biscuits.

EDWINA'S CHICKEN ROLL

Leftover

COOKED or CANNED CHICKEN, at least 1½ cups, chopped

and

Flour, 2 cups
Baking powder, 4 tsp.
Salt, ¾ tsp.
Shortening, margarine, or butter, 3 tbsp.
Milk, ⅔ cup
Melted butter, 2 tbsp.
Finely chopped stuffed olives, ¼ cup

Minced green pepper, 1 tbsp.
Chicken broth, 2 tbsp.
Sherry, 1 tbsp.
Milk, 2 tbsp.
Condensed tomato or mushroom soup, or leftover chicken gravy, plus sherry (optional), 1 tbsp.

Sift flour with baking powder and salt; cut in shortening. Gradually add milk to make a soft dough. Roll lightly in 11 × 4-inch rectangle, ½ inch thick. Brush with melted butter. Mix chicken, olives, green pepper, chicken broth, and sherry. Spread on dough. Roll like jelly roll. Seal edges with dampened fingers. Brush with milk. Bake on greased shallow pan in hot 425° oven 25 minutes or until done. Serve with condensed tomato or mushroom soup or leftover chicken gravy as sauce, plus 1 tbsp. sherry if liked. SERVES 3–4.

Suggested: Serve with Spinach Gnocchi[R], mixed greens salad with French Dressing[R]—and hot buttered biscuits.

POULTRY-STUFFED PEPPERS

Leftover
COOKED CHICKEN or TURKEY, finely diced, 1½ cups
and

Firm green peppers, 4	Minced parsley, 1 tsp.
Beaten eggs, 2	Chutney, 1 tsp.
Milk, 1 cup	Curry powder, ½ tsp.
Salt, 1 tsp.	American cheese slivers, 4
Pepper to taste	tbsp.
Grated onion, 1 small	Boiling water, 1 cup

Cut tops from stem end of green peppers. Remove seeds and fibers. Parboil for 5 minutes. Drain. Prepare filling: mix eggs with milk, salt, pepper, onion, parsley, chutney, and curry powder. Add chicken or turkey. Fill peppers to within ½ inch of top. Sprinkle with cheese. Place in baking dish filled with 1 cup boiling water. Bake in moderate 350° oven until peppers are tender and filling is set, about 35 minutes. MAKES 4 SERVINGS.

Suggested: Serve with Carrot Baked Ring[R], lettuce-to-mato salad with lemon French Dressing[R]—and buttered corn muffins.

MUSHROOM CHICKEN

Leftover
COOKED CHICKEN, at least 1 cup cut in slivers—or 1
8-ounce can
and

Bacon strips, 2, cut in bits	Pepper, ¼ tsp.
Broad noodles, 4 ounces	Condensed cream of
Minced onion, 1 tsp.	mushroom soup, 1 can
Boiling salted water, 2	Water or milk, ½ soup can
quarts	Grated cheese, ¼ cup
Salt, ½ tsp.	Chopped parsley, 1 tsp.

Fry bacon until crisp. Drain and set aside. Cook noodles and onion in boiling water until tender. Drain. Transfer to saucepan. Add salt, pepper, mushroom soup, water, cheese, parsley, and chicken. Cook covered 7 minutes until thoroughly heated. Serve on heated platter. Sprinkle with grated cheese and bacon bits. SERVES 2–3.

Variation: Mix in any leftover peas, carrots, or string beans.

Suggested: Serve with Turnip-Tomato Patty Casserole[R], Asparagus and Olive Salad[R]—and popovers.

SPECIAL BOMBAY CURRY

Leftover
> COOKED or CANNED CHICKEN or TURKEY, cut in large pieces, at least 2 cups

and

Butter or margarine, 2 tbsp.	Sugar, ¼ tsp.
Curry powder, 1 tsp.	Finely chopped onions, 2 medium
Dry mustard (optional), ¼ tsp.	Flour, 2 tbsp.
Cayenne pepper, few grains	Chicken broth, or cubes and boiling water, 1 cup
Salt, ½ tsp.	Lemon juice, 1 tbsp.

Melt butter in saucepan. Add curry powder (more, if you prefer), mustard, cayenne, salt, sugar, and onions. Blend well. Cook slowly until onions are soft. Add chicken. Sprinkle with flour. Cook 10 minutes over high heat until brown. Stir in chicken broth. Cover and simmer lightly another 10 minutes. Just before serving, add the lemon juice. SERVES 4.

Suggested: Serve with fluffy cooked rice. Surround with minced almonds, grated lemon peel, minced hard-cooked egg, pickle, relish, and chutney.

SUPER CHICKEN SALAD

Leftover
COOKED CHICKEN, at least 2 cups; bone, cut in bite-size chunks
and

Sliced celery, ½ cup	Cream, 2 tbsp.
Carrot slivers, ½ cup	Salt, ½ tsp.
Minced green pepper, ¼ cup	Pepper, ⅛ tsp.
	Vinegar, 1 tbsp.
Grated onion, 1 tsp.	Lettuce chunks, 2 cups
Mayonnaise, ⅓ cup	

Toss together all ingredients but lettuce. Chill about 30 minutes. Toss with crisp cold lettuce chunks immediately before serving. SERVES 3–4.

Suggested: Serve with squash soufflé—and toasted corn bread.

FESTA TURKEY-NUT LOGS

Leftover
COOKED TURKEY, at least 1½ cups, finely diced
and

Butter or margarine, 3 tbsp.	Cracker crumbs, 1 cup mixed with ½ cup finely chopped nuts
Flour, 3 tbsp.	
Milk, ¾ cup	Beaten egg, 1, mixed with 2 tbsp. cold water
Salt and pepper to taste	
Chopped onion, 2 tbsp.	Deep fat

Melt butter in saucepan. Blend in flour. Gradually add milk, stirring constantly until thick and smooth. Add salt, pepper, onion, and turkey. Chill several hours or overnight. Shape into 8 1½-inch-thick logs. Roll in crumbs, then in egg, and again in crumbs. Fry in fat 375° until golden. SERVES 3–4.

Variation: Tuck a tsp. of loganberry jam (or any other you prefer) in the center of each log.

Suggested: Serve with Lyonnaise String Beans[R] and tomato-watercress salad with French Dressing[R]—and buttered black bread slices.

LAND O' COTTON POTPIE

Leftover
COOKED TURKEY, at least 1 cup, diced
and

Butter or margarine, 2 tbsp.

Flour, 2 tbsp.

Turkey stock, 2 cups or canned chicken broth

Diced, boiled or leftover ham, ½ cup

Salt and pepper to taste

Corn-bread mix, 1½ cups, prepared as directed

Melt butter in saucepan. Blend in flour. Gradually add stock, stirring constantly until thick and smooth. Add turkey, ham, salt, and pepper. Pour into shallow casserole. Top with prepared corn-bread mix. Bake in medium 375° oven 20–25 minutes until crispy brown. SERVES 2–3.

Suggested: Serve with Kidney Bean Salad[R] and fruit sherbet.

PAT'S STRING BEAN AND BACON SALAD

Leftover
COOKED TURKEY or CHICKEN, diced, at least 2 cups
and

Bacon, 5 slices	Cooked French string
Catsup, 4 tbsp.	beans, 2 cups
Mayonnaise, ½ cup	Diced tomatoes, 4 medium
Vinegar, 2 tbsp.	Chunked lettuce, 1 head
Salt, ½ tsp.	Slivered Swiss cheese, 1
Pepper, ⅛ tsp.	cup

Fry bacon until crisp. Set aside. Mix catsup, mayonnaise, vinegar, salt, and pepper. Add beans, turkey, tomatoes, and lettuce and toss lightly. Chill until serving time. Serve garnished with Swiss cheese and crumbled bacon. SERVES 4.

Variation: Other garnishes: chopped hard-cooked egg, sliced pimentos, chopped olives, or diced pickled peaches.

Suggested: Serve with Baked Bean-Burgers[R]—and hamburger buns.

VERY SPECIAL TURKEY

Leftover
  COOKED TURKEY, diced, at least 1½ cups
and

Cooked broccoli, 1½ cups or 1 package quick-frozen, prepared as directed	Grated cheese, 3 tbsp.
	Sherry, ¼ cup
	Condensed cream of chicken soup, 1 can
Melted butter or margarine, 1 tbsp.	Salt and pepper to taste

Place broccoli in shallow buttered casserole. Sprinkle with butter, 1 tbsp. cheese, and 1 tbsp. wine. Spread turkey over broccoli. Sprinkle with 1 tbsp. cheese and 1 tbsp. wine. Pour chicken soup, salt, and pepper over all. Top with remaining cheese and wine. Bake in moderate 350° oven until piping hot, golden brown, about 15 minutes. SERVES 4.

Suggested: Serve with boiled rice or on hot toast with tossed greens salad and Chive Dressing[R]—plus poppy-seed rolls.

YAMMY TURKEY

Leftover
  ROAST TURKEY, at least 1½–2 cups, chunked
and

Butter or margarine, 3 tbsp.	large, or leftover mashed sweet potatoes
Sliced onions, ½ cup	Hot milk, ½ cup
Turkey gravy or thickened bouillon, 1½ cups	Salt and pepper to taste
	Sherry[S], 2 tbsp.
Boiled sweet potatoes, 4–5	

Substitute: 1 tsp. grated orange rind and 2 tbsp. hot orange juice.

Sauté onions in 1 tbsp. butter until tender. Add turkey and gravy. Turn into shallow baking dish. Peel and mash potatoes with milk, remaining butter, salt, pepper, and sherry. Spoon onto turkey mixture. Bake in medium 400° oven 25 minutes until piping hot. SERVES 3–4.

Variation: Add chunked pineapple to onions.

Suggestion: Serve with a crisp cold mixed greens salad with French Dressing[B]—and French bread.

VEGETABLES

VEGETABLES

Vegetables are the most hated and loved, the most necessary and most mishandled of all foods. It's not their fault. Trouble often begins in childhood when badly cooked, tasteless carrots or overcooked greens are mercilessly shoved between clamped teeth as a parent mutters, "Eat it (you little monster)—it's good for you, darling."

The result is that vegetables play the big role of a "heavy" in childhood, yet often don't get even a "walk-on" in later stages of life.

Of course they're good for you—and they can be delicious, too. Everyone should have at least one and preferably two vegetables daily for necessary God-given vitamins.

In our day of waterless cookers and modern markets which provide all varieties of vegetables throughout the year, this is not actually hard. It requires only a little thought and interest.

Remember also that appearances win half the battle. Interesting colors and textures awaken interest at the table.

For economy, buy fresh vegetables in season, and clean them before storing. Discard wilted and discolored leaves. Store wrapped in waxed paper or in food bags or vegetable crisper in refrigerator. Keep canned vegetables in the pantry shelf. If you've a home freezer or a freezing section in your refrigerator, include frozen vegetables in your staple list.

Throw nothing away. There is a use for even the smallest bit as an addition to soup, salad, or sauce. Check your refrigerator daily.

The following recipes are flexible—more or less vegetables may be used. Substitute fresh, canned, or frozen ones, adjusting cooking time and liquids accordingly.

Basic Cooking Instructions for Vegetables

Fresh Vegetables Wash thoroughly. When possible, cook with skins on. Never overcook. Steaming generally better than boiling—thus, cook tightly covered over low heat in a minimum of water—one inch deep or less if possible. This shortens cooking time, minimizes vitamin loss. Use any leftover liquid to make sauce for vegetables—or use it in canned soups, gravies, and sauces in place of water. Always add vegetables when water is boiling—and keep it boiling. Some like adding monosodium glutamate with seasoning.

Frozen Vegetables Prepare as directed on package. Store in freezing compartment of refrigerator. If less than the whole package is needed, divide it by chopping with ice pick. Keep the rest rewrapped and solidly frozen until required, and use as soon as possible.

Canned Vegetables Buy by brands and quantity needed. Often large sizes are more economical and enable you to plan leftovers. They are ready-cooked, require only heating before serving. Do not waste liquid from can—it is high in food value. Boil liquid down over high heat, then add vegetables, lower heat, add butter and seasoning, and gently reheat—do not recook. Or use liquid as sauce for vegetables. If only part of a can is needed, refrigerate remainder in can, cover tightly, and use as soon as possible.

Leftover Vegetables

QUICK 'N EASYS

VEGETABLE MACEDOINES can be made easily by combining bits of leftover cooked vegetables. They are tasty, economical food stretchers. Keep in mind contrasting colors, textures, flavors, and shapes. All vegetables taste better when seasoned with melted butter.

Try These Combinations:

Peas and carrots

Lima beans and corn
(succotash)

Corn and tomatoes

Beets and celery

Eggplant and diced
tomatoes

Diced potatoes and carrots

Asparagus and tiny pearl
onions

Cauliflower and string
beans

Peas and mushrooms

Baked potato—pinched
open and garnished with
peas or mushrooms

Spinach and potatoes

Spinach and tomatoes

Cauliflower, peas, and
carrots

Beets and broccoli

Soup Garnish: Any combination of cooked vegetables, cut julienne style—that is, in thin matchstick strips—may be used as a soup garnish.

ASPARAGUS AND OLIVE SALAD

Leftover

COOKED ASPARAGUS, at least 1½ cups, cut in ½-inch lengths

and

Mayonnaise, ½ cup

Chopped black olives, 1
tsp.

Chopped pimento-stuffed
olives, 1 tsp.

Salt and pepper to taste

Finely shredded lettuce,
3 cups

Combine mayonnaise, black and stuffed olives with salt and pepper. Arrange asparagus in lettuce nests, topped with salad dressing. THIS MAKES AN ACCOMPANYING SALAD FOR 4.

ASPARAGUS BAKED RING

Leftover
COOKED ASPARAGUS, finely chopped, at least 1 cup
and

Cream, ¼ cup	Salt, ½ tsp.
Cracker crumbs, ¼ cup	Pepper to taste
Butter or margarine, 2 tbsp.	Chopped olives, 2 tbsp.
	Stiffly beaten egg whites, 3
Beaten egg yolks, 3	

Mix cream, crumbs, butter, egg yolks, salt, pepper, and olives with asparagus. Fold in egg whites. Turn into buttered ring mold. Set mold in pan of water. Bake in preheated 350° oven 30 minutes. Turn onto flat plate and fill center with rice or contrasting colored vegetable, if liked. THIS AS A MAIN DISH SERVES 2—AS A SIDE DISH, 4.

ASPARAGUS SOUFFLÉ

Leftover
COOKED ASPARAGUS, diced or cut in 3-inch pieces, 1½ cups
and

Butter or margarine, 3 tbsp.	Whole clove, 1
Sliced onion, ¼ cup	Well-beaten egg yolks, 3
Flour, 3 tbsp.	Salt and pepper to taste
Canned chicken soup or milk, 1 cup	Paprika, dash
	Nutmeg, dash
Bay leaf, 1	Grated Parmesan, 2 tbsp.
	Stiffly beaten egg whites, 3

Melt butter, brown onion, blend in flour. Blend well. Gradually add soup or milk, bay leaf, and clove, stirring

constantly until thick and smooth. Remove from heat.
Add egg yolks, seasoned with salt, pepper, paprika,
nutmeg, Parmesan cheese, and asparagus. Fold in egg
whites. Pour into buttered soufflé dish. Bake in moderate
375° oven 40 minutes. SERVES 4.

Suggested: This plus Lamb Roll[R] makes a hearty meal.

BAKED BEAN-BURGERS

Leftover
  BAKED BEANS, mashed to purée, at least 1½ cups
and

Grated onion, 1 medium	2 tbsp. water and 1 tbsp.
Salt, ½ tsp.	catsup
Pepper, ¼ tsp.	Bread or cracker crumbs,
Tabasco (optional), 2	1 cup
dashes	Shortening, lard, or
Flour, 1 cup	drippings, 1 cup
Beaten egg, 1—mixed with	

Mash beans with onion, salt, pepper, and Tabasco. Shape
into burgers. Dip first into flour, then egg mixture, and
then in crumbs. Fry in fat or drippings until brown.
Drain on absorbent paper before serving. SERVES 3-4.

Suggested: This plus salad of meat slivers, peas, sliced
pineapple, and onion shavings with French Dressing[R]
makes a good menu.

MAIN-LINE BEET SALAD

Leftover
  COOKED BEETS, diced, 1 cup
and

Diced cooked potatoes,	Minced celery, ¼ cup
1½ cups	Pared and diced apples, 2
Chopped onions, ½ cup	Boston lettuce leaves, 4

SOUR CREAM DRESSING:

Mayonnaise, ¼ cup   Sugar, ¼ tsp.
Sour cream, ½ cup   Prepared mustard, ½ tsp.
Salt, ¼ tsp.   Vinegar, 1 tsp.

Combine beets, potatoes, onions, celery, and apples. Prepare the Sour Cream Dressing. Toss with beet-potato combination; chill well. Serve in lettuce cups. MAKES 4 SERVINGS.

Variation: Garnish with hard-cooked egg slices.

Suggested: Serve with Fish Puff Speciale[R]—and buttered pumpernickel slices.

MIXED BEET RING MOLD

Leftover
COOKED BEETS, drained and diced, about 1 cup
and

Lemon gelatin, 1 package   Pared diced apples, 1 cup
Hot water and/or beet   Chopped nuts (optional),
   juice, 1 cup   2 tbsp.
Wine vinegar, 2 tbsp.   Chopped chives, 2 tbsp.
Orange juice, ¾ cup   Crisp chicory lettuce
Salt and pepper to taste   Mayonnaise
Diced celery, ¾ cup

Dissolve gelatin in water or beet juice. Add vinegar, orange juice, salt, and pepper. Mix thoroughly. Chill. When beginning to set, fold in beets, celery, apples, nuts, and chives. Turn into wet ring mold. Chill until set. Unmold and serve, center filled with crisp curly chicory lettuce dressed with mayonnaise. THIS MAKES A FINE SUMMER-DAY MAIN-DISH SALAD FOR 4.

BISBEE BROCCOLI

Leftover
COOKED BROCCOLI, cut in 1½–2-inch lengths—about
15
and

Butter or margarine, 3   Sherry, 3 tbsp.
  tbsp.   Salt and pepper to taste
Flour, 3 tbsp.   Grated Swiss cheese, ⅓
Milk, 1½ cups   cup

Melt butter; stir in flour. Blend well. Add milk and sherry
gradually, stirring until thick and smooth. Add salt and
pepper. Arrange a layer of broccoli in well-buttered small
casserole; cover with hot white sauce; sprinkle with
cheese. Repeat until casserole is full. Top with cheese.
Brown under broiler until bubbly. SERVES 3–4.

Variation: Cover each layer with cooked, diced, leftover
chicken or ham.

GREEN BEAN SALAD BOWL

Leftover
COOKED GREEN BEANS, at least 1½ cups, drained
and

Anchovy fillets, 4–5   Wine vinegar, 1½ tbsp.
Salad oil, ⅓ cup   Grated cheese, ½ cup
Salt, ½ tsp.   Tabasco, dash
Pepper to taste   Shredded lettuce, 2 cups

Mash anchovies in oil; add salt, pepper, vinegar, grated
cheese, and Tabasco. Add green beans. Chill slightly.
Toss with lettuce before serving. THIS MAKES AN AP-
PETIZER OR ACCOMPANYING SALAD FOR 2–3.

BROCCOLI SOUFFLÉ GOURMET

Leftover
COOKED BROCCOLI, at least 1 cup, chopped
and

Butter or margarine, 3 tbsp.	Minced parsley, 1 tsp.
Flour, 3 tbsp.	Worcestershire sauce, 1 tsp.
Cream, ½ cup	Salt and pepper to taste
Rich chicken bouillon, canned or cubes, ½ cup	Nutmeg, pinch
Well-beaten egg yolks, 3	Grated cheese, 4 tbsp.
Grated onion, 1 tsp.	Stiffly beaten egg whites, 4

Melt butter in a saucepan. Blend with flour until smooth.
Gradually stir in cream and chicken bouillon, stirring constantly until thick and smooth. Do not boil. Remove from heat. Stir in egg yolks that have been beaten with the onion, parsley, Worcestershire, salt, pepper, and nutmeg. Add chopped broccoli and grated cheese. Carefully fold egg whites into mixture. Pour into buttered soufflé dish. Bake in medium hot 400° oven 25 minutes. Serve at once. SERVES 3–4.

Suggested: This plus a salad of fennel, sliced potatoes, romaine lettuce, crumbled bacon with French Dressing[B] makes a good luncheon or supper.

MINTED CARROT AND CHICORY SALAD

Leftover
COOKED CARROTS, cut in thin slices, 2 cups
and

Vinegar, ⅓ cup	Salt and pepper to taste
Water or carrot liquid, 3 tbsp.	Chopped chicory, 2 cups
Chopped fresh mint, 1 tsp.	Salad oil, 1½ tbsp.

Marinate carrots in vinegar, water, mint, and seasoning 2 hours or longer. Wash and dry chicory. Sprinkle with oil; toss with well-drained carrots. Taste and add seasoning if necessary. SERVES 4.

CARROT BAKED RING

Leftover
COOKED CARROTS, chopped or finely diced, at least
1½ cups
and

Mayonnaise, ½ cup	Cream, ½ cup
Melted butter, 2 tsp.	Salt, ½ tsp.
Flour, 1 tbsp.	Pepper to taste
Well-beaten eggs, 3	Grated lemon rind, 1 tsp.

Mix mayonnaise, butter, and flour. Add eggs, cream, salt, pepper, and grated lemon rind. Butter ring mold generously. Place carrots around it. Pour in egg mixture. Set mold in pan of water. Bake in preheated 350° oven 30 minutes or until set. Turn onto flat plate and fill center with rice or contrasting colored vegetable, if liked. THIS AS A MAIN DISH SERVES 2—AS A SIDE DISH, 4.

CARROT RAMEKINS

Leftover
COOKED CARROTS, mashed, at least 1½ cups
and

Salt and pepper to taste	Lightly beaten eggs, 1–2
Minced onion, 1 tbsp.	Celery soup, ½ can
Caraway seeds (optional), 1 tsp.	Milk or carrot water, ¼ soup can
Milk or cream, 3 tbsp.	Cayenne, 2 specks

Mix carrots with salt, pepper, onion, caraway seeds, and milk. Stir in eggs. Pour into individual buttered ramekins; place in pan containing hot water. Bake in moderate 350° oven about 30 minutes, or until knife inserted in custard comes out clean. Meanwhile heat celery soup with milk.

Season with cayenne. Invert custards onto hot platter; serve with celery sauce. THIS IS A SIDE DISH—MAKES 3–4 SERVINGS.

Variation: Add a spoonful chopped raw celery or green pepper to sauce.

OVEN CASSEROLE

Leftover
COOKED CARROTS, drained and mashed, at least 1½ cups
and

Cooked rice, 1½ cups	Salt, ½ tsp.
Grated onion, 1 tbsp.	Pepper to taste
Grated cheese, 1 cup	Butter or margarine, 3
Beaten egg, 1	tbsp.

Mix together carrots, rice, onion, grated cheese, egg, salt, and pepper. Turn into shallow buttered casserole. Dot with butter. Bake in moderate 375° oven 35 minutes. THIS AS A MAIN DISH SERVES 2.

Variation: Mix in any leftover peas, mushrooms, or any finely diced meat.

CAULIFLOWER SALAD

Leftover
COOKED CAULIFLOWER, broken into pieces, 1½ cups
and

Salad oil, 4 tbsp.	Paprika, ½ tsp.
Tarragon vinegar, 1 tbsp.	Pepper to taste
Salt, ½ tsp.	Cooked green beans, cut
Sugar, pinch	up (optional)[8], 1 cup
Dry mustard, ¼ tsp.	Torn lettuce, 2 cups
Minced onion, 1 tbsp.	

Substitute: Cooked peas.

Mix salad oil with vinegar, salt, sugar, mustard, onion, paprika, and pepper. Toss in cauliflower and beans. Marinate at least 1 hour. Drain. Serve on torn lettuce leaves. SERVES 4.

Variation: Serve with avocado dressing.

Suggested: Serve with Corn Chowder[B]—and hot buttermilk biscuits.

DEEP-FRY CAULIFLOWER

Leftover
  COOKED CAULIFLOWER, cut in flowerets, about 1½ cups
and

Flour, ½ cup	Milk, ⅓ cup
Baking powder, 1 tsp.	Lemon juice, 2 tbsp.
Salt, ¼ tsp.	Deep-frying fat
Nutmeg, few grains	Lemon quarters, 4
Beaten egg, 1	

Sift flour with baking powder, salt, and nutmeg. Beat egg into milk; blend with flour mixture. Beat with rotary beater until smooth and free of lumps. Just before serving, dip well-drained cauliflower into lemon juice, then into batter, and fry in hot deep fat 375° until golden brown. Drain and serve with lemon quarters. THIS IS A SIDE DISH—MAKES 3-4 SERVINGS.

Suggested: Odd bits of leftover cold cooked fish, meat, poultry, or vegetables dipped into the batter and fried make an Italian *fritto misto.* Add a mixed greens salad, your favorite dressing, and you have a gourmet special.

CURRIED CAULIFLOWER

Leftover
COOKED CAULIFLOWER, at least 1½ cups
and

Butter or margarine, 2 tbsp.	Milk, ¾ cup
Chopped onions, 2 small	Ground ginger, ⅛ tsp.
Flour, 2 tbsp.	Cayenne, 2 specks
Salt and pepper to taste	Parsley, 1 tbsp.
Curry powder, 1 tbsp.	Chutney (optional), 2 tbsp.

Melt butter in saucepan. Cook onions until soft and transparent. Stir in flour, salt, pepper, curry powder; blend well. Add milk gradually, stirring until thick and smooth. Add ginger and cayenne. Add well-drained cauliflower —be careful not to crumble. Simmer gently to reheat cauliflower, about 5 minutes. Serve garnished with parsley and chutney. SERVES 3–4.

Suggested: This served on boiled rice plus a salad of lettuce, tomatoes, and tossed greens—with celery seed and French Dressing[R]—makes a good luncheon snack or Sunday-night supper.

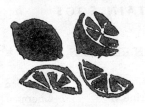

CHICK-PEA SOUP

Leftover
COOKED or CANNED CHICK-PEAS, at least 1½ cups,
plus 1 cup liquid
and

Oil, ⅓ cup	Anchovy paste, 1 tsp.
Minced garlic, 2 cloves	Red pepper (optional), 1
Rosemary (optional), ½ tsp.	tiny pod
	Salt and pepper to taste
Bouillon cubes, 2 dissolved in 1 quart boiling water	Elbow macaroni or vermicelli, broken into
Tomato paste, 1 tbsp.	pieces, 1 cup

Place oil, garlic, and rosemary in soup kettle. Brown well.
Stir 2 cups bouillon gradually into tomato and anchovy
pastes. Add to soup kettle. Simmer slowly 20 minutes.
Add red pepper, chick-peas with liquid, and remaining
bouillon, salt, and pepper. Boil 5 minutes. Add macaroni and cook until tender, about 10 minutes. Taste and
add more pepper if necessary. SERVES 3–4.

Suggested: This plus a salad of greens, okra, green pepper—with French Dressing[R]—makes a good soup and
salad meal.

BLUE MOUNTAIN EGGS

Leftover
COOKED CORN KERNELS, 1 cup
and

Bacon, 6 strips	Chopped pimentos, 2 tbsp.
Butter or margarine, 1 tbsp.	Chopped green pepper, 1 small
Chopped onion, 1 tbsp.	Eggs, 4
Chopped parsley, 1 tbsp.	Salt and pepper to taste

Brown bacon until crisp. Remove and keep warm. Add corn and butter to bacon drippings. Add onion, parsley, pimentos, and green pepper. Stir continuously until brown. Drop in eggs, one at a time. Scramble each until egg is set but not dry. Season. Serve with bacon strips. MAKES 3–4 SERVINGS.

CORN CHOWDER

Leftover
COOKED CORN KERNELS, about 2 cups, plus liquid
and

Finely diced bacon or salt pork, ¼ cup	Boiling water, 2 cups
	Salt, 1 tsp.
Diced onions, 1 cup	Pepper, ¼ tsp.
Flour, 1 tbsp.	Milk, 2 cups
Diced raw potatoes[S], 1 cup	

Substitute: Cooked potatoes, add to chowder same time as corn.

Sauté bacon with onions until bacon is crisp. Sprinkle with flour; blend well. Add potatoes, water, salt, and pepper. Bring to boil. Simmer until potatoes are tender. Add corn and milk; heat thoroughly. SERVES 4.

Variation: Add ¼ cup chopped green pepper with bacon and onions.

Suggested: Serve with Mushroom Chicken[R]—and hot buttered Parker House rolls.

CORN KERNEL PIE

Leftover
COOKED or CANNED CORN KERNELS, at least 1½ cups
and

Butter or margarine, 2 tbsp.
Grated onion, 1 tbsp.
Grated green pepper, 1 tbsp.
Flour, 2 tbsp.
Bay leaf, 1
Milk or bouillon, ¾ cup
Slightly beaten egg yolks,

3, with 1 tbsp. chopped parsley, 1 tsp. Worcestershire sauce, Tabasco, drop, salt and pepper to taste
Stiffly beaten egg whites, 3
Buttered bread crumbs, 2 tbsp.

Melt butter in a saucepan. Sauté onion and green pepper 1 minute. Add flour. Blend until smooth. Add bay leaf. Gradually stir in milk, stirring constantly until thick and smooth. Do not boil. Remove from heat. Remove bay leaf. Stir in egg yolks that have been mixed with the parsley, Worcestershire, Tabasco, salt, and pepper. Add corn kernels, then fold in stiffly beaten egg whites. Turn into buttered baking dish; top with bread crumbs. Bake in medium hot 400° oven 25 minutes. Serve at once. SERVES 3–4.

Suggested: This plus salad of sliced oranges, endive, and onion shavings with French Dressing^R makes a nice light supper.

EGGPLANT SALAD

Leftover
COOKED EGGPLANT, at least 1 cup, peeled and mashed
and

Minced garlic clove, 1
Salt and pepper to taste
Olive oil, 2 tsp.

Lemon juice, 2 tsp.
Chopped parsley, 1 tbsp.
Lettuce cups, 2

Mash eggplant thoroughly. Mix in garlic, salt, pepper, oil, lemon juice, and parsley. Chill thoroughly. Serve in lettuce cups. SERVES 2.

Suggested: This plus Eggs all'Alfredo[R] and garlic bread makes a good Sunday-night supper.

EGGPLANT PARMESAN

Leftover
COOKED EGGPLANT, sliced thin, boiled or fried, at least 2 cups
and

Canned tomato sauce[S], 1¼ cups	Mozzarella, Münster, or Swiss cheese, ½ cup
Parmesan cheese, 3 tbsp.	

Substitute: Tomato Sauce[R].

Sprinkle 2 tbsp. tomato sauce on bottom of shallow casserole. Cover with 1 layer eggplant. Add more sauce, Parmesan, then mozzarella or other cheese. Repeat until all eggplant is used—ending with mozzarella. Bake in medium hot 400° oven 15 minutes. THIS AS A MAIN DISH SERVES 2–3.

Suggested: This as a side dish plus stuffed peppers makes a fine supper menu for 4.

NINO'S WHITE BEAN SOUP

Leftover
COOKED WHITE BEANS, with liquid[S], 2½ cups
and

Garlic clove, 1	Coarsely ground black pepper to taste
Olive oil, 2 tbsp.	
Parsley, 2 tbsp.	Toast, 4 slices, rubbed with 2 slices garlic
Salt to taste	

Substitute: If not enough liquid to cover, add bouillon.

Heat beans with garlic, olive oil, parsley, salt, pepper, and liquid (and/or bouillon) to cover. Place 2 slices garlic-rubbed toast in each soup plate. Cover with beans and be prepared for a delightful gourmet soup meal. THIS MAKES AN APPETIZER SOUP FOR 4 OR A MAIN DISH PLUS SALAD MEAL FOR 2.

KIDNEY BEAN SALAD

Leftover
COOKED KIDNEY BEANS, at least 1½ cups
and

Mashed garlic clove, 1	Sugar, ⅛ tsp.
Salad oil, 4 tbsp.	Lemon juice, 2 tbsp.
Minced onion, 1 tbsp.	Chopped green pepper, 3
Salt, 1 tsp.	tbsp.
Coarsely ground black	Lettuce cups, 4
pepper to taste	Crumbled crisp bacon, 4
Paprika, ⅛ tsp.	slices
Dry mustard, ⅛ tsp.	

Combine garlic, oil, onion, salt, pepper, paprika, mustard, sugar, and lemon juice. Mix well. Add kidney beans and green pepper. Chill several hours. Serve on lettuce cups garnished with bacon. THIS AS AN ACCOMPANYING SALAD SERVES 4—AS A MAIN DISH, 2.

Variation: Add thin slices of cooked frankfurters.

CONCORDIA BEANS AND TUNA FISH

Leftover
COOKED WHITE BEANS, at least 2 cups
and

Coarsely chopped tuna	Minced celery (optional),
fish, 1 cup	1 stalk
Minced onion, 1 small	Minced garlic, 1 clove
Oil, ¼ cup olive or very	Chopped parsley, 1 tsp.
good salad oil	Salt, ½ tsp.
Vinegar, 3 tbsp.	Pepper, ½ tsp.
Basil, ½ tsp.	

Mix all the ingredients well. Taste for seasoning. Add more salt, pepper, vinegar, and/or oil to suit your taste. Allow to stand covered in cool place at least an hour before serving. Stir occasionally. THIS AS A LUNCHEON MAIN DISH SERVES 2—AS A SIDE DISH MAKES 4 SERVINGS.

Variation: Try salmon instead of tuna.

LENTIL CHEESE CASSOULETS

Leftover
COOKED LENTILS, drained, about 1½ cups
and

Sliced onion, 1 large	American cheese cut into
Diced bacon, 3 strips	slivers, ¼ cup
Salt and pepper to taste	Tomato sauce, 1 cup
Lemon juice to taste	

Sauté onion with bacon until bacon is crisp. Add lentils, salt, pepper, and lemon juice. Heat thoroughly. Turn into 3–4 individual casseroles. Top each with American cheese. Brown under broiler until cheese is melted. Serve with tomato sauce. THIS MAKES EXCELLENT SIDE DISH FOR 3–4.

Variation: Top each casserole with 1 slice of tomato; season highly with salt and pepper. Brown under broiler.

LENTIL BROCHETTES

Leftover
COOKED LENTILS, mashed, 1½ cups
and

Butter or margarine, 3 tbsp.	Cayenne, dash
Flour, 4 tbsp.	Grated bread slice, 1
Milk, 1 cup	Flour
Salt, ½ tsp.	Beaten egg, 1, with 1 tbsp. water
Pepper to taste	Bread crumbs
Worcestershire sauce, 1 tsp.	Deep fat

Melt butter, stir in flour. Blend well. Add milk gradually, stirring until thick and smooth. Do not boil. Add salt and pepper, lentils, Worcestershire, cayenne, and grated bread. Cool until easy to handle. Shape into 4-inch cones on brochettes. Roll in flour, then in egg mixture, and finally in bread crumbs. Fry in hot fat, 375°, until golden brown. Drain on absorbent paper before serving. MAKES ABOUT 4 BROCHETTES.

Variation: Shape into round balls—alternate with 1-inch pieces of frankfurters and/or bacon on skewers. Roll in melted butter. Cook under hot broiler 10 minutes.

Suggested: These served with your favorite tomato sauce plus a salad of lettuce cups with cole slaw make a light Sunday-night supper.

SQUASH PIE

Leftover
COOKED SQUASH, mashed, at least 1 cup
and

Toasted bread, soaked in
milk until soft, 2 slices
Slightly beaten eggs, 2
Butter or margarine, 2
tbsp.

Finely chopped onion, 1
Salt, ½ tsp.
Pepper to taste
Cream, 2 tbsp.

Mix bread with squash. Mash until smooth. Add eggs and blend with melted butter, onion, salt, and pepper. Pour into shallow buttered casserole. Sprinkle cream over all. Bake in medium 350° oven 25 minutes until golden brown. SERVES 2–3.

CANADIAN LIMA BEANS

Leftover
COOKED LIMA BEANS, at least 2 cups
and

Chicken stock or bean
liquid, ½ cup
Paprika, ½ tsp.
Worcestershire sauce, 1
tsp.

Cheddar cheese slivers, 1
cup
Canadian bacon slivers[8],
½ cup

Substitute: Bacon strips.

Mix chicken stock with paprika, Worcestershire, and beans. Place in buttered baking dish alternating with layers of cheese. Top with bacon. Bake in moderate 350° oven until bacon is crisp and cheese has melted. SERVES 4.

Variation: Add mushrooms.

Suggested: Serve with cucumbers, chopped spring onions, peas and escarole salad with Blue Cheese Dressing[R] —and hot rolls.

CHEESE, TOMATOES, AND LIMA BEANS

Leftover
   COOKED LIMA BEANS, at least 1½ cups
and

Sliced tomatoes, 4	Diced rattrap cheese, 2
Basil, ½ tsp.	cups
Thinly sliced sweet yellow	Butter or margarine, 1
onion, 1 medium	tbsp.
Salt and pepper to taste	

Arrange alternate layers of tomatoes, sprinkling of basil, Lima beans, onion, salt, pepper, and cheese in small, deep, buttered casserole. Repeat until all the ingredients are used, topping with cheese. Dot with butter; cover. Bake in moderate 350° oven 40 minutes. SERVES 3–4.

Suggested: This plus Coquille St. Jacques[R] makes savory fare.

LIMA BEAN BACON POT

Leftover
   COOKED LIMA BEANS, at least 1 cup
and

Diced bacon, 2 slices	Salt, ½ tsp.
Diced onion, ¼ cup	Pepper to taste
Diced pimentos, 2 tbsp.	Chicken soup, ½ cup

Fry bacon with onion until crisp. Add pimentos, Lima beans, salt, and pepper. Pour into buttered baking dish. Cover with chicken soup. Bake in moderate 350° oven 20 minutes. SERVES 2.

Variation: Add cooked corn kernels.

LIMA BEAN SALAD

Leftover
COOKED LIMA BEANS, at least 1 cup, drained
and

Anchovy fillets, 4	Wine vinegar, 1½ tbsp.
Salad oil, ⅓ cup	Tabasco, dash
Salt, ½ tsp.	Boston lettuce cups, 4
Pepper to taste	Crumbled bacon, 4 strips

Mash anchovies in oil; add salt, pepper, vinegar, and Tabasco. Toss in Lima beans. Chill. Serve in lettuce cups garnished with crumbled bacon. THIS MAKES AN ACCOMPANYING SALAD—SERVES 3–4.

Variation: Add 2 sliced hard-cooked eggs just before serving.

MUSHROOM CROQUETTES

Leftover
COOKED MUSHROOMS, sliced, at least 1 cup
and

Butter or margarine, 3 tbsp.	Crumbled crisp bacon, 2 strips
Flour, 4 tbsp.	Flour
Milk, 1 cup	Beaten egg, 1, with 1 tbsp. water
Salt, ½ tsp.	
Pepper to taste	Bread crumbs
Worcestershire sauce[s], 1 tsp.	Deep fat

Substitute: Sherry, 1 tbsp.

Melt butter, stir in flour. Blend well. Add milk gradually, stirring until thick and smooth. Do not boil. Add salt, pepper, mushrooms, Worcestershire, and crumbled bacon. Cool until easy to handle. Shape into patties, cones, or what pleases you. Dip in flour, then in egg mixture, and finally in bread crumbs. Fry in hot fat, 375°. (A cube of bread will turn brown in 60 seconds.) Drain on paper before serving. MAKES ABOUT 4 CROQUETTES.

Suggested: These served with celery sauce or canned condensed celery soup plus a salad of romaine lettuce, carrot strips, diced green pepper, and French Dressing[R]—make a light meal.

CURRIED PEA SPOON-FRITTERS

Leftover
    COOKED PEAS, at least 1½ cups
and

Flour, 1 cup	Well-beaten egg, 1
Baking powder, 1 tsp.	Milk, ¾ cup
Salt, ½ tsp.	Fat
Curry powder, 1 tbsp.	Lemon quarters, 4

Sift flour with baking powder, salt, and curry powder. Beat egg into milk; blend into flour mixture. Beat with rotary beater until smooth and free of lumps. Add peas. Drop by spoonfuls into ½-inch fat in shallow frying pan. Fry until golden brown. Drain on absorbent paper. Serve with lemon quarters. THIS IS A SIDE DISH—MAKES 4 SERVINGS.

MINTED PEAS IN ONIONS

Leftover
    COOKED GREEN PEAS, 1 cup
and

Large onions, 4	Fresh chopped mint[S], ½
Water, ½ cup	tsp.
Butter or margarine, 2	Milk, ½ cup
tbsp.	Finely chopped parsley,
Flour, 1 tbsp.	½ tsp.
Substitute: Curry powder.	

Parboil onions for 20 minutes. Remove centers, leaving bottom ends intact. Place in shallow casserole with ½ cup water. Brush with 1 tbsp. melted butter, bake until tender and lightly browned in moderate 350° oven about 45 minutes. Melt 1 tbsp. butter in saucepan. Blend in flour until smooth. Add mint; gradually stir in milk, stirring constantly until thick and smooth. Add peas; cook another minute. Fill baked onion shells with creamed peas; dust with parsley. Serve hot. THIS IS A SIDE DISH—MAKES 4 SERVINGS.

Variation: Eliminate mint, chop onion centers, and mix with peas.

QUICK 'N EASY POTATOES

Leftover
  BOILED POTATOES

A

Dress up boiled potatoes with a sauce by blending 1 can condensed cream of mushroom soup with ⅓ cup milk. Heat thoroughly.

B

Or mix potatoes with leftover peas; place in shallow casserole. Pour over 1 can condensed cream of celery soup, mixed with ⅓ cup milk. Sprinkle with American cheese slivers—and pop under broiler till cheese bubbles, potatoes are thoroughly reheated.

C

Slice boiled potatoes; mix with cooked peas, cooked carrots, cooked beets, or what-have-you. Add a little chopped pickle relish and moisten with condensed cream of celery soup, plus lemon juice, salt, pepper to taste. Chill thoroughly. Serve on lettuce leaves.

DELMONICO POTATOES

Leftover

BOILED POTATOES, peeled and sliced, at least 1½ cups
and

Butter or margarine, 2 tbsp.

Chopped onion, 1 tbsp.

Flour, 2 tbsp.

Salt and white pepper to taste

Milk, ¾ cup

Cheddar cheese slivers, ¼ cup

Sliced hard-cooked eggs, 1–2

Buttered bread crumbs, ¼ cup

Melt butter in a saucepan. Sauté onion. Blend with flour until smooth. Season with salt and pepper. Gradually add milk, stirring constantly until thick and smooth. Arrange potatoes, cheese, hard-cooked eggs and white sauce in alternate layers in well-buttered baking dish. Top with buttered crumbs. Bake in moderate 350° oven until well browned. THIS IS A SIDE DISH—MAKES 2–3 SERVINGS.

Variation: Sautéed mushrooms and/or sliced cooked meat may be added to make a hearty main dish.

EVER-WELCOME POTATO SALAD

Leftover

BOILED POTATOES, peeled and diced, at least 2 cups
and

Salad oil, 2 tbsp.

Vinegar, 1 tbsp.

Salt, ½ tsp.

Pepper to taste

Chopped celery, ½ cup

Chopped dill pickle, 3 tbsp.

Chopped scallion, 1

Diced hard-cooked egg, 1

Chopped fresh parsley, 2 tbsp.

Chopped pimento-stuffed olives, ½ cup

Mayonnaise, 4 tbsp.

Mix potatoes with oil, vinegar, salt, and pepper. Chill for ½ hour. Add celery, pickle, scallion, egg, parsley, olives,

and mayonnaise. Blend well. Chill thoroughly. This
MAKES ACCOMPANYING SALAD FOR 4.

MASHED POTATO CHEESE BALLS

Leftover
MASHED POTATOES (WHITE or SWEET), at least 1½
cups
and

Milk, ¼ cup, about	Egg, 1, beaten with 1
Grated cheese, ½ cup	tbsp. water
Salt and pepper to taste	Bread crumbs, 1 cup
Nutmeg, pinch	Deep fat
Cayenne, few grains	

Heat mashed potatoes, milk to moisten, and grated
cheese. Add salt, pepper, nutmeg, and cayenne. Mix
well. Cool. Roll in walnut-sized balls. Dip in egg, then
roll in bread crumbs. Fry in hot deep fat 375° (a cube of
bread will brown in about 60 seconds) until golden
brown. Drain on absorbent paper before serving. This
IS A SIDE DISH—MAKES 2–3 SERVINGS.

Variation: Shape into patties. Place on buttered baking
dish. Sprinkle with milk. Bake in moderately hot oven
until golden.

REAL HASHED BROWN POTATOES

Leftover
BOILED POTATOES, peeled and cut in small dice, at
least 2½ cups
and

Flour, 2½ tbsp.	Pepper to taste
Minced onion, 1 tbsp.	Butter or margarine, 2½
Milk, 3 tbsp.	tbsp.
Salt, ½ tsp.	

Mix potatoes with flour, onion, milk, salt, and pepper.
Heat 2 tbsp. butter in skillet. Turn potato mixture into

skillet; press down with spatula. Cook over medium heat, shaking pan to prevent sticking. Keep pressing down to form brown crusty underside. Remove from pan. Clean out any bits of crust. Melt remaining butter in pan. Return potatoes to pan, crust side up. Continue cooking, shaking pan and pressing down with spatula until crusty brown on both sides. SERVES 4.

SPANISH HASH

Leftover
BOILED POTATOES and ONIONS, diced, enough to make at least 1½ cups
and

Gravy or thickened stock, ¾ cup

Tomato purée, ¼ cup

Butter or margarine, 1 tsp.

Diced pimentos, 2 tbsp.

Chopped green pepper, ¼ cup

Red pepper, 1 tiny pod

Salt to taste

Worcestershire sauce, 1 tsp.

Cooked meat, cut in small dice (optional), 1¼ cups

Bread crumbs, 3 tbsp.

Butter or margarine, 1 tbsp.

Heat gravy with tomato purée and butter. Add pimentos, green pepper, potatoes, onions, red pepper, salt, Worcestershire, and meat. Heat thoroughly. Pour into shallow earthenware casserole. Sprinkle with bread crumbs. Dot with butter. Brown under broiler. SERVES 2.

Suggested: This is good with a tossed greens salad.

SWEET-POTATO PIE

Leftover
BOILED SWEET POTATOES, mashed, at least 1 cup
and

Toasted bread, soaked in milk until soft, 2 slices	Finely chopped onion, 1
	Salt, ½ tsp.
Slightly beaten eggs, 2	Pepper to taste
Butter or margarine, 2 tbsp.	Sherry, 1 tbsp.
	Cream, 2 tbsp.

Mix bread with sweet potatoes. Mash until smooth. Add eggs and blend with melted butter, onion, salt, pepper, and sherry. Pour into shallow buttered casserole. Sprinkle cream over all. Bake in medium 350° oven 25 minutes until golden brown. SERVES 2–3.

Suggested: For a luncheon treat, serve with Sweet and Sour Spareribs[R].

TWICE-BAKED POTATOES

Leftover
BAKED POTATOES, cold, unpeeled, 2
and

Minced garlic, 1 clove	Grated cheese, 1 tbsp.
Salt, ¼ tsp.	Worcestershire sauce, 1 tsp.
Butter or margarine, 1½ tbsp.	

Mash garlic with salt, butter, cheese, and Worcestershire. Slice potatoes almost through in a series of ½-inch-thick diagonals. Spread each section with garlic butter. Bake in shallow pan in moderate 350° oven 25 minutes. SERVES 2.

VEGETABLE PUFFS

Leftover
MASHED SWEET or WHITE POTATOES, at least 1 cup
and

Well-beaten eggs, 2
Flour, ½ cup
Baking powder, 1 tsp.
Salt, ¾ tsp.
Pepper to taste
Nutmeg, dash

Cooked corn kernels, or
  peas or carrots, 1 cup—
  mixed with 1 tbsp.
  grated onion and 1 tbsp.
  chopped parsley
Deep fat

Combine potatoes with eggs and blend thoroughly. Sift
flour, baking powder, salt, pepper, and nutmeg over the
potatoes. Blend well; add vegetable mixture. Drop by
spoonfuls into hot 375° deep fat and (a cube of bread
will turn brown in 60 seconds) fry until golden brown.
THIS IS A SIDE DISH—MAKES ABOUT 8 PUFFS.

Variation: Add either curry or chili powder to taste to
the flour mixture before blending with potatoes.

ALMOND SPINACH CROQUETTES

Leftover
COOKED SPINACH, chopped and drained, at least 1½
cups
and

Butter or margarine, 3
  tbsp.
Flour, 4 tbsp.
Milk, 1 cup
Salt, ½ tsp.
Pepper to taste
Minced toasted almonds,
  2 tbsp.

Worcestershire sauce, 1
  tbsp.
Flour
Beaten egg, 1, with 1 tbsp.
  water
Bread cumbs
Fat

Melt butter, stir in flour. Blend well. Add milk gradually,
stirring until thick and smooth. Do not boil. Add salt,

pepper, spinach, almonds, and Worcestershire. Cool until easy to handle. Shape into patties or cones. Dip in flour, then in egg mixture, and finally in bread crumbs. Fry in deep 375° fat (a cube of bread will turn brown in 60 seconds) until golden brown. Drain on absorbent paper before serving. MAKES 4 GOOD-SIZED CROQUETTES.

Variation: Add mashed potatoes.

Suggested: These served with Cheese Sauce[R] plus potato salad and watercress make a satisfactory supper menu.

CURRIED SPINACH SOUFFLÉ

Leftover
COOKED SPINACH, chopped, 1 cup
and

Butter or margarine, 2 tbsp.	Pepper to taste
Flour, 2 tbsp.	Milk, ¾ cup
Curry powder[S], 1 tbsp.	Beaten egg yolks, 3
Salt, ½ tsp.	Stiffly beaten whites, 3

Substitute: 2 tbsp. minced almonds plus 1 tsp. Worcestershire for the curry.

Melt butter in a saucepan. Blend flour, curry powder, salt, and pepper; add milk; simmer, stirring constantly until thick and smooth. Do not boil. Remove from heat. Stir in egg yolks. Mix well. Add spinach. Carefully fold egg whites into mixture. Pour into buttered soufflé dish. Bake in medium hot 400° oven 25 minutes. Serve at once. SERVES 4.

Suggested: This is good with Super Chicken Salad[R], on a hot summer day.

EGGS À LA TUSCANY

Leftover
COOKED SPINACH or PEAS or STRING BEANS, at least
2 cups
and

Butter or margarine, 2 tbsp.	Milk, 1 cup
	Well-beaten eggs, 4
Finely chopped chives, ⅓ cup	Salt, ½ tsp.
	Pepper, ¼ tsp.
Flour, 2 tbsp.	Chopped black olives, ½ cup
Curry powder, 1½ tbsp.	

Sauté chives in butter. Remove from heat. Add flour and
curry powder. Stir into smooth paste. Return to heat. Add
milk, gradually stirring until thick and smooth. Add eggs,
stir until scrambled. Season with salt and pepper. Place
eggs on heated spinach. Serve garnished with olives.
MAKES 4 SERVINGS.

FLORENTINE RAMEKIN EGGS

Leftover
COOKED SPINACH, chopped, about 1½ cups
and

Eggs, 4–8	Salt and pepper to taste
Heavy cream, 4 tbsp.	Tabasco, dash

Line 4 buttered ramekins or custard cups with spinach.
Break 1 or 2 eggs into each and add 1 tbsp. heavy cream.
Season with salt, pepper, and Tabasco. Bake in moderate
350° oven 10 minutes or until eggs are set. MAKES 4
SERVINGS.

Suggested: Serve with Neapolitan Meat Macaroni[R] to
make a delicious menu for 4.

SPINACH OMELET À LA ROMAINE

Leftover
COOKED SPINACH, 1 cup
and

Beaten eggs, 5
Minced garlic, 1 clove
Cream or milk, 1 tbsp.
Salt, ½ tsp.
White pepper, speck

Butter or margarine, 1½
tbsp.
Anchovy fillets, 8
Tomato sauce, ¼ cup

Heat spinach thoroughly. Drain. Make an omelet: beat eggs briskly with garlic, milk, salt, and pepper. Melt butter in hot frying pan, tipping pan to make sure sides and bottom are greased. Pour in eggs. As eggs begin to set, keep lifting sides and tipping pan to allow uncooked mixture to run under. Continue until eggs are set. Shake pan occasionally to loosen omelet. When bottom is nicely browned and top is consistency of cream, add hot spinach. Fold. Garnish with anchovies. Serve with tomato sauce. SERVES 3–4.

SPINACH GNOCCHI, PRONOUNCED KNEE-OH'-KEY

Leftover
COOKED SPINACH, drained and chopped fine, 1 cup
and

Pot or cottage cheese, ½
pound
Egg, 1
Salt and pepper to taste
Flour, ½ cup

Boiling water, 3 quarts
Butter or margarine, 4
tbsp.
Grated cheese (optional),
4 tbsp.

Mash spinach with cheese, egg, salt, and pepper. Shape into walnut-size balls. Roll in flour. Drop gently into boiling water. When they float to the surface remove with perforated spoon. Drain and serve with melted butter and grated cheese. MAKES 4 SERVINGS.

Suggested: Serve with Ever-Welcome Potato Salad[R] and you've a great meal.

SQUASH PANCAKES

Leftover
   COOKED SQUASH, well drained and mashed, about 1½ cups
and

Salt and pepper to taste	Seasoned flour, 1½ cups
Marjoram, ⅛ tsp.	Beaten egg, 1, mixed with
Grated cheese, 1 tsp.	2 tbsp. water
Grated green pepper, 1 tbsp.	Bread crumbs, 1½ cups
	Bacon drippings, 4 tbsp.

Mix squash with salt, pepper, marjoram, cheese and green pepper. Shape into small flat cakes. Roll in seasoned flour, then in egg, and finally in bread crumbs. Repeat, flour, egg, and crumbs. Fry in hot drippings until brown on both sides. THIS IS A SIDE DISH—SERVES 2–3.

TURNIP-TOMATO PATTY CASSEROLE

Leftover
   COOKED WHITE TURNIPS, 1½ cups, drained and mashed
and

Butter, 3 tbsp.	Condensed mushroom
Sliced tomatoes, 3 medium	soup, ⅔ can
Salt and pepper to taste	Bread crumbs, 2 tbsp.
Marjoram, ⅛ tsp.	mixed with 1 tbsp.
Grated cheese, 1 tbsp.	grated cheese
Beaten egg, 1	Butter, 1 tbsp.

Fry sliced tomatoes in butter. Remove. Mix turnips with salt, pepper, marjoram, and grated cheese. Shape into very thin patties. Dip in egg. Fry in same butter as the tomatoes. Remove. Heat condensed mushroom soup in same pan. Into a baking dish, put one layer of tomatoes, one of turnip patties. Repeat until used up. Pour over mushroom soup. Sprinkle with bread crumbs and grated cheese. Dot with butter. Bake in moderate 375° oven 30 minutes. SERVES 3–4.

Variation: Omit tomatoes. Mash turnips with seasonings. Shape into thick patties. Dip in flour, then in egg, and finally in bread crumbs. Fry in hot bacon fat until brown on both sides.

GERMAN BREAD SOUP

Leftover
COOKED MIXED VEGETABLES, 1½ cups
and

Butter or margarine, ¼ cup	dissolved in 5 cups boiling water
Soft rye bread chunks, 3 cups	Worcestershire sauce, 2 tbsp.
Grated onion, ¼ cup	Nutmeg, ¼ tsp.
Finely chopped parsley, 2 tbsp.	Salt and pepper to taste
Bouillon cubes, 4–	Beaten egg yolks, 2

Melt butter in soup pot. Add bread; mash and fry until brown. Add onion and parsley; stir constantly until onion browns. Pour in bouillon mixed with Worcestershire; add nutmeg. Simmer covered, slowly, about 40 minutes. Add vegetables. Bring to boil. Just before serving season with salt and pepper, then add beaten egg yolks. Stir 1 minute more. SERVES 4–5.

Suggested: Thinly sliced frankfurters make a meal out of this hearty peasant soup.

MIXED VEGETABLE SCALLOP

Leftover
COOKED MIXED VEGETABLES, diced, about 2 cups
and

Butter or margarine, 2 tbsp.	Grated Cheddar cheese, ⅓ cup plus 2 tbsp.
Flour, 2 tbsp.	Worcestershire sauce, 1 tsp.
Salt, ¼ tsp.	
Milk, ¾ cup	Buttered bread crumbs⁸, 1½ tbsp.

Substitute: Crushed corn flakes.

Melt butter; blend in flour and salt. Add milk gradually, stirring constantly until thick and smooth. Add cheese, Worcestershire, and vegetables. Place in shallow buttered casserole. Dot with buttered bread crumbs. Sprinkle with 2 tbsp. grated cheese. Bake in moderate 350° oven 25 minutes until bubbly brown. SERVES 4.

Variation: Pour into individual ramekins.

VEGETABLE-STUFFED PEPPERS

Leftover
COOKED MIXED VEGETABLES, diced, 1½ cups
and

Firm green peppers, 4	Minced parsley, 1 tsp.
Beaten eggs, 2	Worcestershire sauce, 1 tbsp.
Milk, 1 cup	
Salt, 1 tsp.	American cheese slivers, 4 tbsp.
Pepper to taste	
Grated onion, 1 small	Boiling water, 1 cup

Cut tops from stem end of green peppers. Remove seeds and fibers. Parboil for 5 minutes. Drain. Prepare filling: mix eggs with milk, salt, pepper, onion, parsley, and Worcestershire. Add vegetables. Fill peppers to within

½ inch of top. Sprinkle with cheese. Place in baking dish filled with 1 cup boiling water. Bake in moderate 350° oven until peppers are tender and filling is set, about 35 minutes. MAKES 4 SERVINGS.

Suggested: Serve with Beef Mironton[R]—and buttered toasted rye bread.

LYONNAISE STRING BEANS

Leftover
    COOKED STRING BEANS, drained, 1 cup
and

Butter or margarine, 2 tbsp.	Powdered cloves, dash
Minced onion, ¼ cup	Bacon drippings, 2 tbsp.
Minced parsley, 1 tbsp.	Spanish onion, 1, sliced in thin rings
Salt and pepper to taste	

Sauté minced onion in butter until lightly brown—stir frequently. Add string beans, parsley, salt, pepper, and cloves. Cover; simmer very gently 10 minutes. Shake occasionally to keep from burning. Meanwhile—sauté Spanish onion in drippings until brown, then mix with string beans. THIS IS A SIDE DISH—SERVES 2–3.

ODDS-AND-ENDS CASSEROLE

Leftovers

Any three or more of the following sliced, UNCOOKED
VEGETABLES

1–2 turnips, white	2 potatoes
½ cup peas	1–2 carrots
2 tomatoes	½ cup celery

and

Raw rice, ½ cup	Allspice, 1 pinch
Finely sliced onion, 1	Chicken stock, 1½ cups—
Salt, ½ tsp.	use cube, concentrate,
Pepper, ¼ tsp.	or canned

Wash rice and place in alternate layers with vegetables
in deep casserole. Add seasoning. Cover with chicken
stock. Bake tightly covered in moderate 350° oven about
50 minutes, until vegetables and rice are tender. SERVES
2–3.

Variation: Mix in finely diced leftover meats, or add
thinly sliced leftover roast—arranging layers of rice, vegetables, and meat slices. Sprinkle with grated cheese and
bake as above.

Suggested: This plus a salad of chopped celery, mixed
greens with French Dressing[R] makes a meal.

VEGETABLE MACEDOINE SALAD

Leftover
COOKED MIXED VEGETABLES, at least 1½ cups, drained

and

Mashed garlic clove, 1
Salad oil, 4 tbsp.
Salt, 1 tsp.
Pepper to taste
Paprika, ⅛ tsp.
Dry mustard, ⅛ tsp.
Sugar, ⅛ tsp.
Lemon juice, 2 tbsp.

Crumbled blue cheese,
¼ cup
Chopped green pepper, 3 tbsp.
Sliced celery, ½ cup
Broken or torn iceberg lettuce, 2 cups

Combine garlic, oil, salt, pepper, paprika, mustard, sugar, lemon juice, and 3 tbsp. cheese; beat well. Add vegetables, green pepper, and celery. Chill several hours. Serve tossed with lettuce and garnished with remaining blue cheese. THIS AS AN ACCOMPANYING SALAD SERVES 4— AS A MAIN DISH, 2.

VEGETABLE MACEDOINE SALAD

Ingredients:

COOKED MIXED VEGETABLES, at least 1½ cup

and

Minced garlic clove, 1	Crumbled blue cheese, ¼ cup
Salt, 1 tsp.	Chopped green pepper, 2
Pepper to taste	
Paprika, ½ tsp.	Sliced celery, ½ cup
Dry mustard, ¼ tsp.	Broken or torn spinach
Sugar, ½ tsp.	lettuce, 4 cups
Lemon juice, 2 tbsp.	

Combine garlic, oil, salt, pepper, paprika, mustard, sugar, lemon juice, and a dash cheese; beat well. Add vegetables, green pepper and celery; toss. Chill several hours. Serve tossed with lettuce and garnished with remaining blue cheese. This makes a convenient salad starter.

4-6 main dish.

CEREALS
AND PASTES

Leftover Cereals and Pastes

DUTCH NOODLE RING

Leftover
COOKED NOODLES, 2 cups
and

Egg yolks, 2
Milk, ¾ cup
Butter, 1 tbsp.
Salt, ¼ tsp.
Paprika, ⅛ tsp.
Chopped cooked spinach (optional), ½ cup

Worcestershire sauce, 1 tsp.
Catsup, 1 tsp.
Grated Cheddar cheese, ½ cup
Stiffly beaten egg whites, 2

Rinse noodles with boiling water. Drain. Beat egg yolks, milk, butter, salt, and paprika with spinach. Combine with noodles. Mix in Worcestershire, catsup and cheese. Fold in egg whites. Turn into buttered ring mold. Set in pan of hot water. Bake in moderate 350° oven about 40 minutes until set. Serve with Egg Sauce[R], if liked. SERVES 4 AS A MAIN DISH.

Suggested: Serve with a salad of Boston lettuce, chopped fennel, grated carrot with Mustard Dressing[R]—and brown bread and butter.

SPAGHETTI OMELET ALLA MILANESE

Leftover
COOKED SPAGHETTI or MACARONI, 1 cup, cut into
1-inch pieces
and

Butter or margarine, 2 tbsp.	Grated Swiss cheese, 1 tbsp.
Salt, ½ tsp.	Grated Parmesan, 1 tbsp.
Pepper, ¼ tsp.	Tomato sauce, ¼ cup

OMELET INGREDIENTS:

Beaten eggs, 5	
Cream or milk, 1 tbsp.	Butter or margarine, 1½ tbsp.
Salt, ½ tsp.	Grated cheese, 3 tbsp.
White pepper, speck	Tomato sauce, 1 8-ounce can

Melt butter in saucepan. Mix in spaghetti. Season with
salt and pepper. Add grated cheeses and tomato sauce.
Heat thoroughly. Prepare an omelet: beat eggs briskly
with cream, salt, pepper. Melt butter in hot frying pan,
tipping pan to make sure sides and bottom are greased.
Pour in eggs. As eggs begin to set, lift sides and allow
uncooked eggs to run under. Repeat until eggs are set.
Shake pan occasionally to loosen omelet. When bottom
is nicely browned and top is consistency of cream, fill
with spaghetti mixture. Fold. Top with grated cheese.
Serve with tomato sauce. SERVES 3–4.

MACARONI SALAD

Leftover
COOKED MACARONI, at least 2 cups
and

Mayonnaise, ¼ cup
Chili sauce, 1 tsp.
Finely chopped celery, 1 tsp.
Finely chopped red pimento, 1 tsp.
Finely chopped green pepper, 1 tsp.
Chopped hard-cooked egg, 1 tsp.

Salt and pepper to taste
Whipped cream, ½ cup
Sliced radishes, 5
Minced parsley, 1 tbsp.
Pared, chopped cucumber, ½ cup
Slivered American cheese, ½ cup
Chicory lettuce

Mix mayonnaise with chili sauce, celery, pimento, green pepper, egg, salt, and pepper. Carefully fold in whipped cream. Add macaroni, radishes, parsley, cucumber, and American cheese. Chill about 1 hour. Serve on lettuce leaves. THIS MAKES A MAIN DISH SALAD FOR 3–4.

Variation: Cut ½-inch slice from stem end of 4 extra-large firm tomatoes. Scoop out pulp with teaspoon, leaving tomato intact. Chill upside down about 15 minutes. Sprinkle inside with salt and fill with macaroni salad.

MARIA'S SPAGHETTI PIE

Leftover
SPAGHETTI and MEAT BALLS, 3 cups, chopped coarsely
and

Olive oil, 1 tbsp.
Chopped onion, 1 small
Tomato sauce, ¾ cup
Grated Parmesan, 3 tbsp.

Piecrust mix, 1 package, prepared as directed for 2-crust pie
Milk, 2 tbsp.

Sauté onion in oil until brown. Add tomato sauce, spaghetti, and meat balls. Heat 5 minutes. Sprinkle with grated cheese. Add salt and pepper if needed. Line 8-inch piepan with pastry. Pour in spaghetti mixture. Cover with remaining pastry. Pinch edges together. Slash to allow steam to escape. Brush with cold milk. Bake in hot 425° oven 20 minutes or until brown. THIS MAKES MAIN COURSE FOR 3–4.

Variation: Add leftover peas or string beans to spaghetti mixture.

Suggested: Serve with tossed greens salad and you have a company meal.

MING SHRIMP FRIED RICE

Leftover
  COOKED RICE, at least 1½ cups
and

Oil, 2 tbsp.	Shelled and deveined raw
Diced bacon, ¼ pound	shrimp, ½ pound
Minced garlic clove, 1	Beaten egg^s, 1 or 2
Minced onions, 2 medium	Soy sauce, 2 tbsp.
Green pepper, cut in strips,	
⅓	

Substitute: If you've only egg whites, these will do, too.

Brown bacon in oil. Add garlic and onions. Cook 2 minutes. Add green pepper. Cook 2 minutes more. Add shrimp. Cook until pink. Add rice. Stir in eggs until thoroughly blended. Add soy sauce. SERVES 3–4.

INDIAN RICE OMELET

Leftover
COOKED RICE, 1 cup
and

Oil, 1 tbsp.	Well-beaten eggs, 5
Chopped onion, 1 medium	Butter or margarine, 4
Curry powder, 1½ tbsp.	tbsp.
Cream, 2 tbsp.	Cayenne, dash

Fry onion in oil until soft. Stir in curry powder and cream. Remove from pan and stir into eggs. Melt 2 tbsp. butter in omelet pan. Pour in egg mixture. As eggs begin to set, lift sides and allow uncooked eggs to run under. Repeat until eggs are set. Shake pan occasionally to loosen omelet. When bottom is nicely brown and top is consistency of cream, fill with rice that has been sautéed lightly in 2 tbsp. butter seasoned with a dash of cayenne. Fold over. Serve on warm platter. SERVES 3–4.

SPICY RICE SALAD

Leftover
COOKED RICE, at least 1½ cups
and

Mayonnaise, ¼ cup	Diced and drained, cooked
Thick sour cream, ¼ cup	or canned beets, 1 cup
Prepared mustard, ¼ tsp.	Onion shavings, 2 tbsp.
Horseradish, 1 tbsp.	Crisp torn lettuce, 2 cups
Salt and pepper to taste	

Mix mayonnaise with sour cream, prepared mustard, horseradish, salt, and pepper. Toss in rice, beets, and onion shavings. Chill. Serve with broken lettuce leaves. THIS MAKES AN ACCOMPANYING SALAD FOR 4 OR A MAIN DISH FOR 2.

SOUR CREAM EGGS

Leftover
  COOKED RICE, 1½ cups
and

Butter or margarine, 1½ tbsp.

Finely chopped onion, 1 small

Minced garlic, 1 clove

Tomato paste, 2 tsp.

Sour cream, ¾ cup

Salt, ½ tsp.

Pepper, dash

Paprika, ¼ tsp.

Finely chopped chives, 1 tsp.

Chopped parsley, 1 tsp.

Finely chopped capers, 1 tsp.

Eggs, 4

Grated cheese, ¼ cup

Butter, 2 tsp.

Milk, 2 tbsp.

Cook onion and garlic in butter until soft but not browned. Stir in tomato paste and sour cream. Cook until boiling and lower heat. Season with salt, pepper, and paprika. Stir in chives, parsley, capers, and cooked rice. Turn into buttered baking dish. With bottom of water glass make 4 deep depressions in the rice mixture. Break an egg into each, and sprinkle grated cheese over all. Dot with butter, and sprinkle with milk. Bake in moderate 375° oven 15 minutes or until eggs are set and cheese has melted. SERVES 4.

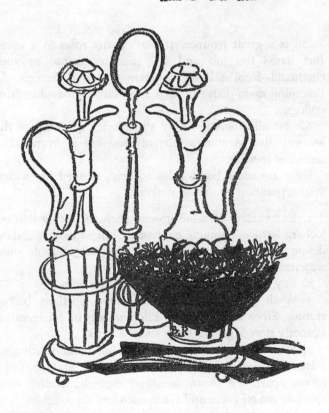

SALAD DRESSINGS

Salad is a great trouper. It plays many roles in a meal. Just name the job and it'll run the gamut at your command—from a light, appetizing opener through the thumping main-dish solo to a final wispish tossed or fruit epilogue.

Almost all salads are easy all-embracing friends of the leftover dish. Any new bits of food are welcome. The more the merrier.

Here are some basic rules to help, if need be, widen your reputation as a salad maker:

1. Buy variety of salad greens. Include Boston lettuce, iceberg lettuce, spinach, cabbage, Chinese cabbage, dandelion greens, endive, chicory, romaine, escarole, and watercress.

2. Buy fresh crisp greens—avoid brown edges.

3. Wash thoroughly; remove wilted portions before storing. Store in crisper or Pliofilm bag in refrigerator. Properly stored, greens keep about a week.

4. To wash, cut out core, hold head under running water allowing spray to enter core-end and so force leaves apart. To clean romaine, escarole, endive, and spinach, cut off cores and clean each leaf thoroughly.

5. Dry greens between towel or in French drier. Wet greens cannot hold dressing, taste flat.

6. Dress salad just before serving to avoid wilting.

7. Never drown salad—put extra dressing on table to allow for individual tastes.

8. Salad leaves must be thoroughly chilled and served on chilled plates.

9. Experiment with different color combinations; gayer salads make gayer appetites.

10. Salads are like swimming in a pool. Remove all obstacles: olive pits, bones, seeds, etc.

11. To insure crisp celery soak with lemon slice in ice water an hour or more.

12. Dressing up ingredients also helps: cucumbers may be fluted by pulling the prongs of a fork lengthwise down a young tender unpeeled cucumber, then slicing thin. Peel paper thin curls of raw carrots. Crisp them in ice water. Small cheese balls cut with potato scoop make tasty garnish.

13. Dip tomatoes in boiling water and out again; skins peel off easily.

And a last word to the wise—salad dressings depend on personal likes and dislikes. The amounts and proportions given here are standard but may be varied to suit your taste. Both French dressing and mayonnaise referred to may be home prepared or store bought.

French Dressings

French dressing is a great favorite in its pure form and an invaluable base for many delicious dressings. Salad-loving families often make up a pint at a time, though some gourmets insist it should be made only when needed, or at the table. However you do it, remember French dressing combines more easily when its ingredients are cold. If you mix directly in the bowl, add oil before vinegar—otherwise vinegar wets greens, causing oil to roll off.

Basic French Dressing I

	For ½ cup	For ¾ cup	For 2 cups
Oil	⅓ cup	½ cup	1½ cups
Vinegar or lemon juice	2 tbsp.	3 tbsp.	½ cup
Salt	½ tsp.	¾ tsp.	1½ tsp.
Pepper	⅛ tsp.	¼ tsp.	½ tsp.

Mix well. For storing, pour ingredients into jar. Shake vigorously until well blended. Store covered on lowest shelf of refrigerator. Shake before using. If desired, rub salad bowl with garlic. If mixing at the table, use 3 parts oil to 1 part vinegar (or lemon), this depending upon individual taste.

Basic French Dressing II

Add following ingredients to above.

	For ½ cup	For ¾ cup	For 2 cups
Dry mustard	¼ tsp.	⅓ tsp.	1 tsp.
Cayenne	1–2 grains	2 grains	3 grains
Garlic	½ clove	1 clove	2 cloves

Allow garlic to stand in dressing for several hours or longer if possible.

American Cheese Dressing To ¾ cup French Dressing I, add 1½ tbsp. catsup, pinch sugar, 1½ tsp. Worcestershire, dash Tabasco, and ¼ cup grated American cheese. Salt and pepper to taste. Beat until creamy. MAKES ABOUT 1 CUP.

Blue Cheese or Roquefort Dressing To ¾ cup French Dressing II, add 3 tbsp. blue or Roquefort cheese. Beat until smooth. Add vinegar or lemon juice if more tartness is desired. (Optional: Rub bowl with cut garlic clove.) MAKES ABOUT 1 CUP.

Caesar Salad Dressing Prepare ½ cup French Dressing II using lemon juice instead of vinegar. Add 1 beaten raw egg, 4 tbsp. grated Parmesan cheese. Serve on tossed salad greens. Add 1 cup bread cubes that have been browned in garlic and oil. Season with freshly ground black pepper. MAKES ABOUT 1 CUP.

Chiffonade Dressing To ¾ cup French Dressing I, add 1 chopped hard-boiled egg, 1 tsp. grated onion, 1 tsp. finely chopped parsley or chervil, 1 tbsp. minced pimento, dash paprika. Mix thoroughly. MAKES ABOUT 1 CUP.

Chive Dressing To ¾ cup French Dressing II, using lemon juice instead of vinegar, add additional 1 tsp. lemon juice, 1 tbsp. chopped chives.

Cream Cheese Dressing Prepare 1 cup French Dressing I, using lemon juice. Beat ½ cup of the dressing into 2½ tbsp. cream cheese mixed with 1 tbsp. chopped chives. Beat until semi-liquid. Add other ½ cup dressing. Mix thoroughly. MAKES ABOUT 1¼ CUPS.

Mustard Dressing To ¾ cup French Dressing I, add 2 tbsp. prepared mustard, 1 tsp. grated cheese. Blend thoroughly. MAKES A LITTLE MORE THAN ¾ CUP.

Vinaigrette Dressing To ¾ cup French Dressing I, add 1 chopped hard-boiled egg, 1 tsp. chopped chives, and 1 tsp. chopped parsley. Serve very cold. MAKES ABOUT 1 CUP.

Cucumber Dressing Mash ½ cup peeled, seeded, grated cucumber with 1 3-ounce package cream cheese. Add 4½ tbsp. oil, 2 tbsp. lemon juice, ½ tsp. salt, dash cayenne, 1 tbsp. minced onion. Mix well. MAKES ABOUT 1 CUP.

Hot Bacon Dressing Fry 2 or 3 slices bacon until crisp. Remove. Crumble. Stir 1 tbsp. flour into fat. Add 2 tbsp. vinegar, ¼ cup boiling water, ½ tsp. dry mustard, ½ tsp. salt, dash cayenne, drop Tabasco, 1 tsp. Worcestershire. Bring to boil. Add bacon. Serve hot over cold salad. MAKES ABOUT ½ CUP.

Sour Cream Dressing Mix 1 cup thick sour cream with 2 tbsp. tarragon vinegar, 1 tsp. finely chopped chives, pinch sugar, salt, cayenne to taste. Serve very cold. MAKES A LITTLE MORE THAN 1 CUP.

Mayonnaise Dressings

Mayonnaise Dressing, like French, is a great favorite as it is—or as a base for countless other dressings. Here, too, many families find it saves trouble to make up one pint at a time. When mixed properly, mayonnaise (unlike French dressing) is not likely to separate. If separated, it can generally be returned to proper consistency by slowly beating in one egg yolk. Homemade or store-bought, *do not* keep it in the coldest part of refrigerator.

Basic Mayonnaise

	For ½ cup	For 1 cup	For 2 cups
Dry mustard	¼ tsp.	½ tsp.	1 tsp.
Sugar (optional)	¼ tsp.	½ tsp.	1 tsp.
Cayenne	1 grain	2 grains	4 grains
Salt	¼ tsp.	½ tsp.	1 tsp.
Egg	1 yolk	1 yolk	1 whole or 2 yolks
Oil	6 tbsp.	¾ cup	1½ cups
Vinegar or Lemon juice	1 tsp.	1 tbsp.	2 tbsp.

Ingredients should be at room temperature. Mix mustard, sugar, cayenne, salt, and egg in deep bowl. Beat thoroughly. Add oil, 1 tbsp. at a time while beating briskly and constantly, until half the oil has been used. Add remaining oil 2 tbsp. at a time. Add lemon juice or vinegar last. *Note:* Eggs must be strictly fresh and not cold. Adding oil too rapidly curdles mayonnaise. Remedy this by beating one egg yolk, then gradually adding curdled mixture until it returns to proper consistency. Then continue adding remaining oil and lastly, the vinegar.

Cucumber Dressing To ½ cup mayonnaise, add 1 small peeled chopped—then drained—cucumber. Mix well. If desired add 1 tsp. tarragon vinegar for extra tartness. Chill thoroughly. MAKES ABOUT ⅔ CUP.

Egg Dressing To 1 cup mayonnaise, add 1 tbsp. chopped pimento, 1 chopped hard-boiled egg, and 1 tbsp. India relish. MAKES ABOUT 1¼ CUPS.

Horseradish Dressing To 1 cup mayonnaise, add 3 tbsp. prepared horseradish plus 2 dashes Tabasco and fresh ground black pepper. MAKES A LITTLE MORE THAN 1 CUP.

Piquante Dressing To 1 cup mayonnaise, add 1 tsp. each finely chopped sour pickles, chives, onion, capers, and pitted green olives. Mix in 1 tsp. prepared mustard. MAKES ABOUT 1 CUP.

Russian Dressing
A

To 1 cup mayonnaise, add 3 tbsp. chili sauce, 1 tbsp. India relish. Makes about 1¼ cups.

B

To ½ cup mayonnaise, add 2½ tbsp. chili sauce, 1 tbsp. minced green pepper, 1 tbsp. chutney, 2 drops Tabasco, ¼ tsp. paprika, 1 finely chopped hard-boiled egg. Mix well. MAKES ABOUT ¾ CUP.

Seafood Dressing To ½ cup mayonnaise, add 3 tbsp. cream, 2 tbsp. catsup, 1 tbsp. lemon juice, 5 drops Tabasco, pinch salt. Mix well. MAKES ABOUT ¾ CUP.

Sour Cream Dressing To ½ cup mayonnaise, add 1 cup thick sour cream, ½ tsp. salt, ½ tsp. sugar, 1 tsp. prepared

mustard, and 2 tsp. vinegar. Mix well. MAKES ABOUT 1½
CUPS.

Tartar Dressing (or Sauce) To 1 cup mayonnaise, add 2
tbsp. chopped gherkins, 1 tbsp. capers, 1 tbsp. chopped
parsley, and 2 tbsp. chopped pimento-stuffed olives. (Optional: Add ¼ cup sherry wine.) MAKES ABOUT 1½ CUPS.

Cole Slaw Dressing Beat 1 egg lightly. Blend with ¼ cup
vinegar, ¼ cup water, 1 tsp. honey, ½ tsp. salt, dash pepper, 1 tsp. prepared mustard. Stir constantly over low heat
until thickened. Cool. MAKES ABOUT ¾ CUP.

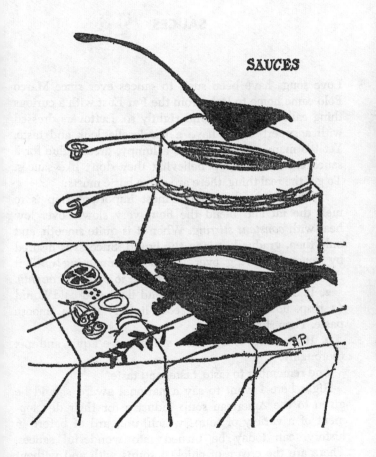

SAUCES

SAUCES

Love songs have been sung to sauces ever since Marco Polo came home to Italy from the Far East with a curious thing called spaghetti. And rightly so. Leftovers dressed with a superb sauce have a Cinderella look and taste. Yet too many people mistake a lumpy, greasy glue for a sauce and so wind up believing they don't like sauces. To get the real thing, there are a few basic musts:

1. The first and probably most important step is to melt the fat and blend the flour very slowly over low heat with *constant stirring*. When it is quite smooth, and only then, gradually stir in the liquid. Success is insured by *constant stirring* over low heat—simmering until it thickens and then allowing the sauce to *cook thoroughly*.

2. If the sauce is too thin, blend flour and cold liquid (1 tbsp. flour to 1½ tbsp. cold liquid) until a smooth paste. Then stir into sauce.

3. If the sauce is too thick, stir in more liquid and mix thoroughly.

And remember to taste, taste, and taste.

Right here I want to say a national award should be given to the American soup industry for their development of a variety of soups which, unheard of before in history, can today be turned into wonderful sauces. There are the cream of chicken soups with and without rice to enhance ham bits, variety meats, eggs, etc. Cream of celery, black bean, mushroom, asparagus, pea, and tomato are good on rice, spaghetti, all kinds of meat, fish, and eggs. Beef consommé can be used for jellied leftover meats or sauce-extenders. Chowders, pepper pots, beef and scotch broth will go wherever your imagination leads you.

And don't forget the canned tomato, spaghetti, barbecue, tartar, hot, cocktail, and bottled meat sauces.

Of course, use them. Better still, learn what wonderful allies they are. Experiment, combining with your leftovers. Add them to your own concoctions. Use them as sauce-stretchers, or as bases for egg dishes. Keep concentrated beef and chicken bouillon always handy. Water never adds anything to a dish—bouillon adds both taste and nourishment.

A sauce's garnish is like a boutonniere and a new spring bonnet. It perks up the wearer. There's a sprinkling of chopped egg yolk, croutons, grated nutmeg, paprika, or toasted almonds. For new taste touches there are bacon crumbs, caraway seeds, paper-thin lemon slices, mint, and so on.

Use your imagination and you're bound to be greeted with admiration.

Aioli Sauce Mash 3–5 or more garlic cloves very smooth with 1 egg yolk, ½ tsp. salt, ¼ tsp. pepper. Add ¾ cup good salad oil, 1 tbsp. at a time, beating well until thick like mayonnaise. Add 1 tbsp. lemon juice. Beat again. MAKES 1 CUP.

Barbecue Sauce Sauté 1 medium minced onion in 1 tbsp. butter until tender. Add ½ cup catsup, 2 tbsp. Worcestershire, ½ tsp. chili powder, ¼ tsp. salt, dash Tabasco, ½ cup water. Bring to boil. An excellent basting sauce. MAKES A LITTLE MORE THAN 1 CUP.

Béarnaise Sauce Boil rapidly ¾ cup dry white wine with ¼ cup tarragon vinegar, 1 tbsp. finely chopped shallots, 1 tsp. chopped parsley, ¼ tsp. tarragon, ¼ tsp. thyme, ⅛ tsp. black pepper—no salt, until reduced to half volume. Strain. Beat in 3 egg yolks, one at a time, alternating with as much slightly melted butter as necessary to keep sauce the consistency of mayonnaise. MAKES ABOUT 1 CUP.

Béchamel (White Sauce)

Thin	*Medium*	*Thick*
1 tbsp. butter	2 tbsp. butter	3 tbsp. butter
1 tbsp. flour	2 tbsp. flour	3 tbsp. flour
Speck pepper	Speck pepper	Speck pepper
½ tsp. salt	½ tsp. salt	½ tsp. salt
1 cup milk	1 cup milk	1 cup milk

Melt butter in double boiler. Stir in flour, pepper, salt, until well blended. Add milk gradually, stirring constantly until thickened. Continue stirring 10 minutes to allow flour to cook. MAKES 1 CUP.

Brown Butter (*Beurre Noir*)   Cook ½ cup butter in saucepan until it foams and becomes light brown. Remove from heat. Add 2 tbsp. lemon juice, ¼ tsp. salt, speck pepper. (Optional: Add 2 tbsp. each chopped parsley, chives.) MAKES ABOUT ½ CUP.

Brown Sauce   Simmer in 3 tbsp. butter in double boiler 1 tsp. minced parsley, 1 minced medium onion, until golden brown. Proceed as for Medium Béchamel, adding flour, pepper, salt—but substituting bouillon for milk. MAKES 1 CUP.

Cheese Sauce   Make 1 cup Medium Béchamel. Stir in ½ cup grated processed cheese until melted. (Optional: Stir in 1 tbsp. prepared mustard, *or* 1 egg yolk, *or* 2 tbsp. chopped green pepper.) MAKES ABOUT 1½ CUPS.

Cocktail Sauce   Mix ⅔ cup chili sauce with 1 tbsp. grated horseradish, 1 tbsp. lemon juice, ⅓ tsp. salt, few grains cayenne pepper, ½ tsp. Worcestershire, 2 drops Tabasco. Chill thoroughly. MAKES ABOUT ¾ CUP. (Optional: Mix with ½ cup mayonnaise.)

Cream Gravy, Poultry   Blend 3 tbsp. poultry drippings with 3 tbsp. flour. Stir in 1 cup sweet cream. Stir until thickened and flour is cooked, about 10 minutes. MAKES ABOUT 1 CUP.

Deviled Sauce   Place ½ cup wine vinegar with ½ tsp. black pepper, 5 red pepper seeds (optional) in saucepan. Simmer until vinegar is reduced to half quantity. Add 1 cup bouillon, 1 tsp. tomato paste. Simmer 10 minutes. Blend 1 tbsp. butter with 1 tbsp. flour. Add to sauce little by little. Stir and heat well. Do not boil. MAKES ABOUT 1 CUP.

Drawn Butter   Blend 3 tbsp. butter with 3 tbsp. flour over low heat. Season with ½ tsp. salt, ⅛ tsp. pepper. Stir in 1½ cups vegetable water. Boil 5 minutes. Add 1 tbsp. butter and 1 tsp. lemon juice. Stir constantly another 5 minutes. MAKES A LITTLE MORE THAN 1½ CUPS.

Egg Sauce   To 1 cup Medium Béchamel or Drawn Butter, add 2 chopped hard-boiled eggs and 1 tsp. finely chopped parsley. MAKES ABOUT 1¼ CUPS.

Hollandaise Sauce   Place 2 egg yolks in a bowl with 1 tbsp. cream, 2 tbsp. tarragon vinegar, dash salt, cayenne pepper. Put the bowl over a deep pan of warm water—do not allow bowl to touch water. Stir constantly over low heat— *do not allow water to boil,* otherwise sauce cooks too rapidly and may curdle. Stir until yolks just begin to thicken. Add about ½ cup butter very slowly, beating constantly until thick. Stir in 1 tbsp. lemon juice.

Mustard Sauce   To 1 cup either Drawn Butter Sauce or Medium Béchamel, add—just before serving—1 tbsp. prepared mustard. Blend thoroughly. Heat but do not boil. Serve at once.

Tomato Sauce   Heat 2 tbsp. olive oil, butter, or lard in a saucepan. Add 1 finely chopped garlic clove, 1 chopped large onion, 1 tbsp. chopped celery, ½ tsp. minced parsley, 1 tbsp. finely chopped carrot. Cook a few minutes, stirring constantly until light brown. Add 1 No. 2½ can tomatoes or 3 cups fresh tomatoes cut in pieces, 1 bay leaf, ½ tsp. basil, ¼ tsp. orégano, ½ tsp. salt, and ½ tsp. pepper. Bring to a boil. Lower heat and simmer for 40 minutes until thick. *Note:* Celery, parsley, and orégano are optional. A pinch of sugar may be added.

Vinaigrette Sauce   To ½ cup French dressing, add 1 tbsp. grated onion, 1 tsp. each chopped parsley, chives, capers, shallots, and gherkins. Warm in top of double boiler over boiling water. Just before serving add 1 tbsp. finely chopped hard-cooked egg. Season with salt and pepper.

NOTHING IN THE HOUSE BUT

"NOTHING IN THE HOUSE BUT——"

When Old Mother Hubbard had a bare cupboard, she really had a bare cupboard and nothing could help her but a shopping expedition.

Because a *bare* cupboard means just that. Yet if your shelf has some stale bread and onions, or maybe a few potatoes and cooking lard, it's far from bare.

True, it can be a problem, as anyone knows who has turned about from what seems to be nothing on the shelf to face a gang of hungry people piling in the front door.

This is what we call the "nothing-in-the-house-but" problem. It's a sort of first cousin to the leftover problem —perhaps more urgent since leftovers can be leisurely scheduled for clever uses. Here, instead, you are asked to meet a sudden demand with what seems to be nothing but unconnectable odds and ends on a pantry shelf.

In short it is "emergency" cooking complicated by what seems to be nothing on hand. Turned to victory, such a challenge very often is more successful and draws greater applause than a carefully prepared dinner.

The main idea is not to be timid. There is no need to be. There are hundreds of ways to prepare emergency dishes out of "nothing"—granting always that a well-stocked pantry averts a serious problem.

For example, there are few odds and ends or leftovers which cannot be thrown together to make a hearty, peasant-type soup to save money and the impossible situation. Certainly the famous Gratinée[R] from the markets in Lyons, or French Onion Soup[R] with garlic-rubbed day-old bread takes no special ingredients that couldn't be found in the barest of larders.

And why limit the imagination to soups?—from Piñon Rice[R] to Potato Latkes[R] there are countless variations. Some are simple as well as real gourmet specialties.

Nothing in the House but Bread

BOUILLON WITH CRUMB BALLS

Nothing in the house but
BREAD CRUMBS, ⅓ cup
and

Bacon or meat drippings, 2 tbsp.
Grated lemon rind, 1 tbsp.
Salt and pepper to taste
Fine chopped parsley, 1 tbsp.

Grated onion, 1 tbsp.
Egg white, 1
Bouillon cubes[S], 2, dissolved in 2 cups boiling water

Substitute: Any soup or broth or stew.

Mix bread crumbs with drippings, lemon rind, salt, pepper, parsley, onion, and egg white. Form into tiny marble-sized balls. Just before serving, drop into hot soup. SERVES 2.

GRATINÉE LYON

*Nothing in the
house but*
  BREAD, 6 stale hard rolls, or 6–8 or more thick pieces of
  stale bread
and

Butter or margarine, 2
  tbsp.
Bouillon, cubes, canned, or
  concentrate, 6 cups
Bay leaf, 1
Chopped parsley, 1 tbsp.
Salt and pepper to taste

Nutmeg, few grains
Grated cheese, ½ cup
Eggs (optional), 1–4
Cognac, rum, red wine,
  sherry, etc. (optional)
  4 tbsp.

Break bread into small pieces. Melt butter in saucepan.
Add bread and fry until golden. Pour in hot bouillon.
Add bay leaf, parsley, salt, pepper, and nutmeg. Cover
and simmer gently 25 minutes. Discard bay leaf. Season
to taste. Pour into 4 individual casseroles. Sprinkle each
with 2 or 3 tbsp. cheese. Brown under broiler about 8
minutes. If you've eggs, slip 1 well-beaten egg into each
casserole just before serving. Add a good tbsp. cognac,
rum, or sherry, etc., to each. THIS IS A GOOD LATE-WINTER-
NIGHT WARMER FOR 4.

Variation: Pour into 1 large serving casserole. Add all the
cheese. Brown under the broiler. Slip 1 beaten egg only
into the soup just before serving. (Do not stir soup after
the egg has been added.)

4

NEAPOLITAN BROCHETTES

Nothing in the
house but

STALE BREAD, 12 thick slices, preferably French or
Italian bread

and

CHEESE, Swiss, Edam, Münster, or Processed American,
½ pound

and

Tiny firm tomatoes   Flour, 1 cup
    (optional), 4   Lightly beaten egg, 1
Milk, ½ cup, seasoned   Oil, lard, or fat, 1 cup
    with salt and pepper

Cut bread (crusts removed) and cheese into 1 × ½-inch
pieces. String on 8 skewers alternating bread, cheese,
tomatoes—repeating until skewers are filled. Dip into
milk, then flour, then egg. Fry in hot oil until golden
brown on all sides. THIS CAN BE MAIN DISH FOR 4.

Variation: Eggplant, zucchini, leftover boiled or canned
potatoes, parboiled onions, and/or bacon may be added.

Nothing in the House but Canned Fish

FISH AU GRATIN

*Nothing in the
house but*
   TUNA or SALMON, 7-ounce can
and
   AMERICAN CHEESE, ¼ cup, grated
and

Chopped onion, 2 slices mixed with 3 tbsp. butter or margarine and 1 tbsp. chopped green pepper (optional)	Salt and pepper to taste
	Milk[8], 1½ cups
	Mustard, ½ tsp.
	Lemon juice, 1 tbsp.
Flour, 3 tbsp.	Bread crumbs, 3 tbsp.
	Butter, 1 tbsp.

Substitute: Evaporated milk and water—or chicken soup or bouillon cube and boiling water.

Cook onion, butter, and green pepper over very low heat 5 minutes. Stir in flour and salt and pepper. Add milk gradually, stirring constantly until thick and smooth. Flake fish if necessary. Add to mixture with mustard and lemon juice. Fill buttered ramekins or baking dish. Top with cheese mixed with bread crumbs. Dot with butter. Bake in moderate 350° oven 15 minutes until well browned. SERVES 4.

FISH FLAKE SPAGHETTI

*Nothing in the
house but*
   CANNED TUNA or CRAB MEAT and/or SALMONˢ,
   1 or 2 cans
and
   SPAGHETTI, 1 pound
and

Oil, ¼ cup	Sherry (optional), ½ cup
Chopped onion, ¾ cup	Tomato sauce, 1 cup or
Minced garlic, 2 cloves	diced tomatoes, 6, and
Minced parsley, 1 tsp.	water or bouillon, ½
Chopped celery	cup
(optional), 1 tbsp.	Boiling water, 4 quarts,
Salt, ½ tsp.	seasoned with 3 tbsp.
Pepper, ¼ tsp.	salt
Paprika, ¼ tsp.	Butter, 2 tbsp.

Substitute: Any leftover boiled or baked fish, boned and
flaked.

Prepare sauce before cooking spaghetti. Brown onion,
garlic, parsley, and celery in oil. Add salt, pepper, paprika, tomato sauce, fish (flaked and boned), and sherry.
Simmer 5 minutes. (If using tomatoes, add with water
or bouillon before adding fish flakes and sherry. Simmer
30 minutes, then add fish flakes and sherry and simmer
5 minutes.) Boil spaghetti in salted water until *al dente*
(firm, not too soft). Serve sauce over well-drained hot
spaghetti. Top with butter. THIS MAKES A FILLING MAIN
COURSE FOR 4.

IRISH SCALLOPED TUNA CASSEROLE

Nothing in the
house but
CANNED TUNA or SALMON, 1 7-ounce can
and
UNCOOKED POTATOES, pared and thinly sliced, 2½
cups
and

Butter or margarine[81], 3 tbsp.	Pepper to taste
Flour, 3 tbsp.	Minced green pepper (optional), 1 tbsp.
Milk[82], 1½ cups	Minced parsley (optional), 1 tbsp.
Minced onion, 1 medium	
Salt, ½ tsp.	

Substitute[1]: Fish oil or salad oil.
Substitute[2]: Evaporated milk and water.

Boil potatoes in salted water 10 minutes. Drain. Melt butter in saucepan; blend in flour. Add milk gradually, stirring constantly until thick and smooth. Add onion, salt, pepper, green pepper, and parsley. Arrange potatoes and fish (flaked and boned) in alternate layers in buttered casserole. Pour sauce over all. Bake in moderate 350° oven 40 minutes. THIS MAKES A FINE UNEXPECTED-COMPANY DISH FOR 4–5.

Variation: Add chopped stuffed olives to the white sauce.

NEWBURG ROLLS

*Nothing in the
house but*
  CANNED FISH, 1 No. 2 can
and
  HARD CRUST ROLLS, 4
and

Butter or margarine, 3 tbsp.	Worcestershire sauce, ½ tsp.
Flour, 4 tbsp.	Tabasco, dash
Milk, 1½ cups, or ¾ cup evaporated milk and ¾ cup water	Sherry (optional), 3 tbsp.
	Lemon juice, ½ tsp.
	Paprika

Melt butter in saucepan; blend in flour. Add milk gradually, stirring constantly until thick and smooth. Add Worcestershire, Tabasco, sherry, lemon juice, and fish, flaked and boned. Cut off thin slice from top of each roll. Scoop out insides. Pile fish and sauce into each. Dust with paprika; brown quickly under broiler. SERVES 4.

Variation: Add mushrooms to sauce. This can be served on toast, rice, or noodles. Anyway you serve it, it makes savory fare.

PANTRY SHELF FISHBIT

Nothing in the
house but
CANNED SARDINES or SALMON or CRAB MEAT or
TUNA, about 1 cup
and

Butter or margarine, 2
    tbsp.
Flour, 2 tbsp.
Dry mustard, ½ tsp.
Salt and pepper to taste
Milk, 1 cup, or ½ cup
    evaporated milk and ½
    cup water

Grated cheese or cheese
    slivers, ½ cup
Worcestershire sauce, ½
    tsp.
Toast, 3–4 slices

Melt butter in saucepan; blend in flour, mustard, salt,
and pepper. Add milk gradually, stirring constantly until
thick and smooth. Add cheese and Worcestershire. Stir
until cheese melts. Add canned fish, flaked and boned.
Heat thoroughly. Serve on toast. MAKES 3–4 SERVINGS.

PANTRY SHELF PANCAKE CASSEROLE

Nothing in the
house but
CANNED TUNA or SALMON or CRAB MEAT, 1
7-ounce can
and

Canned cream of
    mushroom, celery, or
or
Butter or margarine, 2
    tbsp.
and
Worcestershire sauce, ½
    tsp.
Chopped parsley, 1½
    tbsp.

    tomato soup, 1 can
Milk, ¼ cup

Flour, 2 tbsp.
Milk⁸, 1 cup

Salt and pepper to taste
Grated cheese, ¾ cup
Pancake mix, 1 cup
Milk, 1 cup

Substitute: ½ cup evaporated milk and ½ cup water.

If using canned soup, add ¼ cup milk, ½ tsp. Worcestershire, parsley, salt, pepper and half cup cheese. Add canned fish, flaked and boned. Heat. *Otherwise,* prepare a sauce by melting butter in saucepan; blend in flour. Add milk gradually, stirring constantly until thick and smooth. Add Worcestershire, parsley, salt, pepper, half cup grated cheese, and fish flakes. *Then:* Make the pancakes as directed on package. Follow basic recipe or add a beaten egg. Then place a layer of pancakes in shallow baking dish. Place a dab of fish sauce in center of each. Cover with remaining pancakes. Top with remaining sauce. Garnish with remaining grated cheese. Bake in medium hot 400° oven ten minutes. THIS IS A WONDERFUL SUNDAY-NIGHT SNACK FOR 4.

SARDINE CROQUETTES

Nothing in the
house but

SARDINES, 1 3¼-ounce can
and

Butter or margarine, 2 tbsp.	Minced parsley, 1 tbsp.
Flour, 2 tbsp.	Beaten egg, 1
Milk, ½ cup	Crushed corn flakes, ½ cup
Bread crumbs, ¾ cup	Fat or shortening
Salt and pepper to taste	Lemon wedges, 4
Worcestershire sauce, ½ tsp.	

Melt butter in saucepan; blend in flour. Gradually add milk, stirring constantly until thick and smooth. Mash sardines into sauce; add 4 tbsp. bread crumbs, salt, pepper, Worcestershire, and parsley. Chill half hour or longer. Shape into croquettes. Roll in remaining bread crumbs, then in egg, and then in corn flakes. Fry in fat,

½ inch deep, until golden. Serve with lemon wedges.
Good with Cocktail Sauce[R] or Tartar Sauce[R]. MAKES 4
GOOD-SIZED CROQUETTES.

SARDINE ENVELOPES

*Nothing in the
house but*
   SARDINES, 2 cans, 3¼ ounces
and
   Piecrust mix, 1 package

Prepare piecrust as directed on package. Separate sardines. Drain. Lay sardines on pastry—allowing ¾ inch all
around. Cut out each pastry square and fold like en-
velope over sardine. Pinch together with wet fingers and
bake in hot 425° oven 15 minutes. Serve hot. THIS
MAKES ABOUT 15–18 TIDBITS.

SEAFOOD BURGERS

*Nothing in the
house but*
   CLAMS, 1 8-ounce can, minced with liquid
and
   EGGS, beaten, 2
and

Fine cracker crumbs[S], 1 cup	Tabasco, 2 drops
	Bacon drippings, 3 tbsp.
Salt, ¼ tsp.	Burger buns, 6
Pepper to taste	

Substitute: ½ cup cracker crumbs, ½ cup mashed potatoes.

Combine clams, eggs, cracker crumbs, salt, pepper, and
Tabasco. Drop by large spoonfuls into hot bacon drippings, flattening slightly. Brown both sides. Serve on

burger buns spread with Cocktail Sauce[R] or Tartar Sauce[R]. MAKES 6 SERVINGS.

SPANISH TUNA AND OLIVES

Nothing in the
house but

TUNA, 1 can

and

OLIVES, 1 can or jar

and

Butter or margarine, ¾ tbsp.	Lemon juice, 2 tsp.
	Pepper to taste
Flour, ¾ tbsp.	Lemon rind, ½ tsp.
Sherry or white wine, ½ cup	Chopped parsley, 1 tbsp.

Melt butter in a saucepan. Blend in flour. Add sherry, lemon juice, and pepper. Cook, stirring constantly until thick and smooth. Add tuna, lemon rind, and olives. Heat thoroughly. Garnish with parsley. MAKES 3–4 SERVINGS.

Suggested: Served with boiled rice it makes a good meal.

TUNA CHOWDER

*Nothing in the
house but*
    TUNA, 1 can solid pack plus oil
and
    POTATOES, diced and pared, 1 cup
and

Diced bacon, 1½ slices	Canned tomatoes
Thyme, ¼ tsp.	(optional)[s], No. 1 can
Diced onion, ¼ cup	Water and milk to make
Salt, 1 tsp.	one quart
Pepper to taste	Butter or margarine, 2 tsp.
	Minced parsley, 1 tsp.

Substitute: 3 medium tomatoes cut in slivers, plus ½ cup
water.

In deep kettle, sauté bacon until crisp. Add oil drained
from tuna. Stir in thyme and onion. Cook until soft. Add
potatoes, salt, pepper, and tomatoes. Cook covered 15
minutes until potatoes are tender. Add water and milk,
then tuna, broken into pieces. Cook another 5 minutes.
Serve topped with dabs of butter and minced parsley.
SERVES 3–4.

Nothing in the House but
Cereals and Pastes

GARLIC MACARONI

*Nothing in the
house but*
    MACARONI or SPAGHETTI, 1 pound
and

Boiling salted water, 4	Basil, ¼ tsp.
quarts	Parsley, 1 tbsp.
Garlic, 15–20 cloves	Salt and pepper
Olive oil, 4 tbsp.	

Boil macaroni in salted water until *al dente* (firm, not too soft). Now for the sauce: This is a recipe for the more adventurous. If you like garlic, you're in for a real treat. If you're the timid type, use only 15 garlic cloves—but not less. Cook the garlic in the oil with basil and parsley until they are fried golden brown and soft. Mash all together to make a smooth paste. Season to taste. Mix well. Toss with boiled, drained macaroni. Serve in preheated casserole—no cheese!

This is the kind of dish you must share with good friends or spend the evening alone. (And it may be worth it at that.) THIS CAN BE MAIN COURSE FOR 4—GOOD WITH CRISP, COLD SALAD.

Variation: Add 1½ cups canned, leftover, or prepared tomato sauce to garlic paste.

BLACK SPAGHETTI

Nothing in the
house but
　SPAGHETTI, 1 pound
and
　BLACK OLIVES, 1–2 jars pitted
and

Boiling salted water, 4
　quarts
Olive oil or very good
　salad oil, 3 tbsp.
Finely chopped onions, 2
　medium
Chopped garlic, 2 cloves

Bacon (optional), 4 slices
　cut into bits
Chopped anchovy fillets
　(optional), 5, or an-
　chovy paste, 2–3 tsp.
Chopped parsley, 3 tbsp.
Grated cheese, 4 tbsp.

Boil spaghetti until *al dente* (firm, not too soft). Sauté onions in 2 tbsp. oil. Add garlic, olives, bacon, anchovies or anchovy paste, and parsley. Cook until bacon is crisp. Place drained spaghetti in serving dish with remaining

oil. Mix well. Cover with sauce. Serve with grated cheese.
SERVES 4.

Suggested: This plus a salad makes a good meal—wonderful with Gamay Rosé wine.

SPAGHETTI AND GREEN SAUCE

*Nothing in the
house but*
   SPAGHETTI, 1 pound
and

Boiling salted water, 4 quarts	Chopped fresh parsley[8], ½ cup
Olive or good salad oil, 6 tbsp.	Black pepper, ¼ tsp.
Finely chopped garlic, 4 cloves	Butter or margarine, 2 tbsp.
	Grated cheese

Substitute: Chopped spinach or dried parsley.

While spaghetti is boiling in salted water, sauté garlic in oil until golden. Add parsley and black pepper. Simmer a few minutes. When spaghetti is *al dente* (firm, not too soft), drain thoroughly and pour into a heated bowl with the butter. Add the sauce, mix thoroughly. Serve sprinkled with grated cheese. SERVES 4.

SPAGHETTI ALLA POMPIERI

*Nothing in the
house but*
   SPAGHETTI, 1 pound
and

Boiling salted water, 4 quarts	Tabasco, 2 drops
Chopped bacon, ½ cup	Olive oil, 1 tbsp.
Chopped onion, 2 tbsp.	Salt, ¼ tsp.
Chopped green pepper (optional), 3 tbsp.	Pepper to taste
	Grated cheese

While spaghetti is boiling in salted water, fry bacon, onion, green pepper, and Tabasco together until golden brown. Add oil, salt, and pepper. Simmer a few minutes. When spaghetti is *al dente* (firm, not too soft), drain thoroughly and pour into a heated bowl. Add the sauce; mix thoroughly. Serve sprinkled with grated cheese. SERVES 4.

SPAGHETTI ALLA CARBONNARA

Nothing in the house but
  SPAGHETTI, 1 pound
and
  BACON[s], about 8–10 slices, cut in pieces
and

Boiling salted water, 4 quarts	Beaten eggs, 1–2
	Grated cheese, ½ cup
Olive oil, 1 tbsp.	Salt and pepper to taste
Tiny red pepper, 1 pod	Melted butter, 4 tbsp.
Orégano (optional), pinch	

Substitute: If you've less bacon include leftover drippings.

While spaghetti is boiling in salted water, fry bacon with olive oil, red pepper, and orégano until bacon is rich brown (add drippings if to be used). Remove pepper pod. Place large serving bowl over hot water. Beat eggs in bowl until frothy. Add cheese, salt, and pepper. Mix well, then stir in butter and bacon plus oil. When spaghetti is *al dente* (firm, not too soft), drain well and add to bacon mixture. Toss well at table. Serve with additional grated cheese. SERVES 4.

GNOCCHI SEMOLINA, PRONOUNCED KNEE-OH'-KEY

*Nothing in the
house but*
FARINA, 1½ cups quick cooking
and

Water, ¾ cup	Grated cheese, ¾ cup
Milk[81], 2 cups	Butter or margarine, 3
Salt, 2 tsp.	tbsp.
Nutmeg, pinch	Milk, 2 tbsp.
Well-beaten egg[82], 1	

Substitute[1]: Use more water if you've not enough milk.
Substitute[2]: If you've no eggs, use ¼ cup more farina.

Bring water and milk to boil. Add salt. Stir in farina very
gradually to avoid lumps, stirring constantly over low
heat until mixture is quite thick and smooth. Remove
from heat. Stir in nutmeg, egg, and ½ cup grated cheese.
Mix thoroughly. Pour onto lightly floured breadboard.
Spread into sheet ½ inch thick. Cool. Cut into squares.
Arrange in layers in shallow buttered casserole. Sprinkle
each layer with 2 tbsp. grated cheese. Top with dots of
butter. Sprinkle with milk. Bake in moderate 375° oven
15 minutes. This can be prepared in advance. The baking
can wait for the last minute. There is no fixed tradi-
tion about sauces—tomato, cheese, or mushroom, as you
like it. (See Sauces.) THIS CAN BE A MAIN DISH FOR 2
OR AN APPETIZER OR SIDE DISH FOR 4.

PIÑON RICE

*Nothing in the
house but*
  RAW WHITE RICE, 1½ cups
and
  MIXED NUTS, chopped, ⅓ cup
and

Butter or margarine, 3 tbsp.	White pepper, dash
Salt, 1½ tsp.	Canned chicken broth or bouillon, 3 cups

Melt butter in heavy skillet. Stir in rice; cook very slowly until golden; stir occasionally. Season with salt and pepper. Add boiling chicken broth and chopped nuts. Place clean cloth over skillet. Cover tightly—place weights on pot cover. Cook, simmering, very very slowly until rice is tender, about 20 minutes. SERVES 4.

Variation: Add sautéed-in-butter, canned, dried, or fresh mushrooms.

SPANISH RICE MOLDS

*Nothing in the
house but*
  RAW WHITE RICE, 1 cup
and
  CANNED TOMATO SAUCE[S], 1½ cups
and

Boiling salted water, 2 quarts	Sliced black olives (optional), ½ cup
Fat, 2 tbsp.	Chili powder to taste
Sliced onion, 1 large	Salt to taste
Diced green pepper (optional), 3 tbsp.	Sliced green olives (optional), 8

  Substitute: Tomato Sauce[R].

Pick over rice, wash and boil rapidly, in 2 quarts salted water until tender. Drain. Press into 4 buttered ramekins. Set in shallow pan of hot water. Cook 10 minutes on top of stove. Meanwhile, heat fat; sauté onion until golden. Add green pepper, black olives, tomato sauce, chili powder, and salt. Heat 5 minutes. Unmold rice on serving plate. Top with sauce and garnish with green olives. MAKES 4 SERVINGS.

Nothing in the House but Cheese

CHEESE CROQUETTES

*Nothing in the
house but*
   POT CHEESE or COTTAGE CHEESE, 1 cup
and

Grated cheese, 2 tbsp.	Salt, ¼ tsp.
Slightly beaten egg, 1	Pepper, ⅛ tsp.
Flour, 3 tbsp.	Oil, lard, or butter, ½ cup

Mix cheeses, egg, flour, salt, and pepper. Knead on floured pastry board until firm and holds its shape. Form into walnut-sized balls. Fry in hot oil until golden brown on all sides. Drain on absorbent paper. Serve on gaily colored toothpicks. MAKES ABOUT 20. THIS CAN MAKE A MAIN COURSE FOR 2.

Suggested: For a luncheon main dish serve with sauce.

CHEESE BLINTZES

*Nothing in the
house but*
   COTTAGE or POT CHEESE, 2 cups
and

Beaten egg yolk, 1	Milk, 1½ cups
Salt, ¼ tsp.	Flour, 1 cup
Sugar, ¼ tsp.	Stiffly beaten egg white, 1
Melted butter or margarine, ½ tsp.	

FILLING:

Butter or margarine, 1 tbsp.

Beaten egg, 1

Sugar, 1 tbsp.

Beat egg yolk with salt, sugar, butter, and milk. Add flour; stir briskly until batter is smooth. Fold in egg white. Butter 6-inch skillet very lightly. Pour in a very thin layer of batter—just enough to cover bottom of pan. Cook on one side only until golden brown. Turn onto wax paper. Repeat until batter is used up.

Prepare filling: Mix cheese, butter, egg, and sugar. Spoon a heaping tbsp. of filling onto the fried side of each blintz. Fold two sides into filling, then one end over other. Fry in butter until brown. SERVES 4 AS A MAIN DISH.

Suggested: Serve with sour cream.

GOLDEN WELSH RAREBIT

Nothing in the house but

AMERICAN CHEESE[s], 1 cup grated, ¼ pound

and

Butter or margarine, 1 tbsp.

Milk, ½ cup, or ¼ cup plus ¼ cup white wine

Salt, ½ tsp.

Dry mustard, ½ tsp.

Paprika, ¼ tsp.

Worcestershire sauce, ½ tsp.

Slightly beaten eggs (optional), 1–2

Bread, 6 slices

Substitute: Any sharp cheese.

Beat butter, milk, salt, mustard, paprika, Worcestershire, and egg together until well mixed. Stir in grated cheese. Butter bread slices. Cut in half to form triangles. Arrange around edge of shallow pie plate—point side out. Place remaining slices on bottom of plate, butter side down. Pour cheese mixture over all. Bake in moderately hot 400° oven 25 minutes. THIS CAN BE SUPPER MAIN COURSE FOR 2. OR AN APPETIZER OR SIDE DISH FOR 4.

Suggested: Wonderful with cold dry white wine.

POT CHEESE PANCAKES

*Nothing in the
house but*
    POT CHEESE or COTTAGE CHEESE, ½ cup
and

Flour, ¾ cup	Slightly beaten eggs, 2
Baking powder, 1 tsp.	Milk, ¾ cup
Baking soda, ¼ tsp.	Lemon juice, 2 tsp.
Sugar, 1 tbsp.	Grated lemon rind, 2 tsp.
Salt, ½ tsp.	

Sift flour, baking powder, soda, sugar, and salt together.
Mix eggs with cheese, milk, lemon juice and rind. Stir
into flour mixture—do not overmix. Pour from small soup
ladle onto lightly greased griddle. Bake until bubbles begin to form on surface and pancakes become dry looking.
Turn with broad spatula—do not turn more than once.
Good with fried apple slices. MAKES ABOUT 10 PANCAKES.

Nothing in the House but Eggs

BREAD CRUMB OMELET

*Nothing in the
house but*
    EGGS, 4 or 5 separated
and
    SOFT BREAD CRUMBS, 1½ cups
and

Boiling milk, 1¾ cups	Chopped chives or onion,
Salt, ½ tsp.	2 tbsp.
Pepper, ¼ tsp.	Butter or margarine, 2
Cayenne, dash	tbsp.
Powdered clove, dash	

Beat bread crumbs with boiling milk. Add well-beaten
egg yolks. Season with salt, pepper, cayenne, and clove.

Beat until smooth. Stir in chopped chives. Fold in stiffly beaten egg whites. Melt butter in heavy skillet. Add egg mixture. Cook over low heat until bottom and edges of omelet are delicate golden brown and top is puffy—about 7 minutes. Finish cooking in moderate 325° oven 15 minutes or until top is dry. MAKES 3–4 SERVINGS.

Variation: This is wonderful topped with cold cottage cheese, folded over, and served on a hot platter.

EGGS ALL'ALFREDO

Nothing in the house but
  EGGS, 2–4
and

Olive oil, ½ cup
Salt and white pepper to taste
Rosemary or tarragon, pinch
Catsup, 2 tbsp.

Tabasco, 3 dashes
Sliced Cheddar cheese, or any processed cheese, 2–4 thin slices
Bacon (optional), 2 slices

In 2 cup-sized, heat-proof casseroles, place 4 tbsp. olive oil. Warm lightly. Drop in each casserole one or two unbeaten eggs, salt, pepper, rosemary or tarragon, 1 tbsp. of catsup, 3 dashes Tabasco, and the cheese. Cover. Cook over very low heat until done. If using bacon, sauté until crisp. Just before serving, pour off extra oil from each casserole and sprinkle with crumbled bacon. SERVES 2.

Variation: Use one small heat-proof casserole. Top with any leftover bits of meat or poultry.

EGGS À LA SUISSE

Nothing in the
house but
   EGGS, 4
and
   SWISS CHEESE, ½ cup, cut in thin slivers
and

Grated Swiss cheese, 2 tbsp.	Chopped chives, 1 tbsp.
Salt, ½ tsp.	Minced onion, 1 tbsp.
White pepper, ¼ tsp.	Butter or margarine, 2 tbsp.
Chopped parsley, 1 tbsp.	

Sprinkle grated cheese over bottom of shallow buttered casserole. Add eggs; take care not to break yolks. Season with salt and pepper. Carefully cover with cheese slivers, parsley, chives, and onion. Dot with butter. Bake in moderate 350° oven until browned, about 15 minutes. MAKES 4 SERVINGS.

EGGS À LA TRIPE

Nothing in the
house but
   EGGS, 3, hard-boiled, peeled, and sliced
and
   ONIONS, 3, large, sliced
and

Butter or margarine, 2½ tbsp.	Cayenne, speck
Flour, 1½ tbsp.	Nutmeg, dash
Milk, ¾ cup	Grated cheese, 1 tbsp.
Salt, ¼ tsp.	Bread crumbs, ½ tbsp.
Pepper, pinch	Butter or margarine, 1 tsp.

Cook onions in 1 tbsp. butter over low heat until soft. In another pan melt 1½ tbsp. butter. Blend in flour. Add milk and stir until thick and smooth. Season with salt, pepper, cayenne, nutmeg. Place alternate layers of onions, sliced eggs, and sauce in small greased baking dish. Top with grated cheese, a sprinkling of bread crumbs. Dot with butter. Brown under broiler. THIS CAN BE MAIN COURSE FOR 2. OR SIDE DISH FOR 4.

Variation: Any leftovers—meat, fish, chicken, or vegetables—may be added. After stirring milk until thick and smooth, add leftovers and continue as directed.

EGG CURRY

Nothing in the house but

EGGS, 4, hard cooked and sliced

and

CANNED TOMATOES⁸, 1 No. 2 can

and

Butter or margarine, 1 tbsp.	Curry powder, 1 tbsp.
Chopped onion, 1 small	Salt, 1 tsp.
Chopped green pepper, ¼ cup	Sugar, pinch
	Dry mustard, ¼ tsp.
Minced parsley, 1 tbsp.	Boiling water, ½ cup

Substitute: 5 medium fresh tomatoes, cut in slivers, plus extra ½ cup boiling bouillon or water—or

If you've no tomatoes: Blend in 2 tbsp. flour when adding curry. Gradually stir in 1 cup milk, bouillon, or water, stirring constantly until thick and smooth. Add eggs. Cook as directed.

Sauté onion, green pepper, and parsley in butter. Blend in curry powder, salt, sugar, dry mustard. Add tomatoes and boiling water. Stir until well blended and very smooth. Reduce heat. Add eggs. Cover. Simmer very gently—about 15 minutes. SERVES 3–4 AS A MAIN COURSE.

Variation: Add cooked peas or mushrooms, and serve on toast.

Suggested: Served on boiled rice this makes a meal.

EGGS PARMENTIER

Nothing in the
house but
   EGGS, 4
and
   BOILED POTATOES, 6 medium
and

Butter or margarine, 4 tbsp.	Salt, ½ tsp.
	Paprika, ¼ tsp.
Milk^s, ¾ cup plus hot milk for potatoes	

Substitute: Cream or evaporated milk.

Mash boiled peeled potatoes with 3 tbsp. butter and enough hot milk to make smooth and creamy. Arrange in a shallow greased baking dish. With bottom of water glass, make 4 deep depressions in potato. Break an egg in each depression. Pour milk over all. Season with salt, paprika, and dot with remaining butter. Bake in moderate 375° oven until lightly browned and eggs are set, about 15 minutes. MAKES 4 SERVINGS.

Variation: Place a slice of fried ham in each potato depression, then add egg. Sprinkle with grated cheese before placing in oven.

PIPERADE

Nothing in the
house but
   EGGS, lightly beaten, 3–4
and
   TOMATOES, 1 No. 2 can or 4–6 chopped fresh
and

Bacon drippings, 2 tbsp. (or lard, oil, or other drippings)	Salt, ½ tsp. Coarsely ground black pepper, ½ tsp.—less if you can't take it
Sliced onions, 2 large	
Pimento (optional), 1 small can	

Sauté onions in drippings until soft. Add pimento, tomatoes, and salt. Cook covered until purée consistency—
about 30 minutes. Add coarsely ground black pepper.
Stir in beaten eggs and cook, stirring until eggs scramble.
Makes 3–4 servings.

Suggested: This is a meal in itself when served with rice
and bacon strips.

Nothing in the House but
Miscellaneous Vegetables

LIMA BEAN BAKE

*Nothing in the
house but*
   DRIED LIMA BEANS⁸, 2 cups
and

Water, 1½ quarts
Bacon or meat drippings,
   3 tbsp.
Chopped onions, 3
   medium
Diced celery (optional),
   ¼ cup

Brown sugar, 1 tbsp.
Dry mustard, 1 tsp.
Salt, ½ tsp.
Chicken stock, 1 cup
Bacon or pork (optional),
   6 slices

Substitute: 2 No. 2 cans Lima beans. Bake 30 minutes.

Pick over and wash beans. Place in pot with water. Bring
to boil. Boil about 3–4 minutes. Remove and allow to
stand 1 hour. This is a good quick-tenderizing method.
Then mix bacon drippings, onions, celery, sugar, mustard,
salt, and chicken stock. Pour over beans. If using bacon,
top beans with bacon strips. Bake covered in 350° oven
for 2½ hours. SERVES 4 HUNGRY PEOPLE.

ODDS-AND-ENDS VEGETABLE SOUP

*Nothing in the
house but*
   RAW CARROTS, ONIONS, and POTATOES, grated, 1 or
   2 each
and

Boiling water, 5 cups
Bouillon cubes, 2 (or
   concentrate)
Peeled pitted and chopped
   tomatoes (optional), 2
Salt and pepper to taste

Butter or margarine, 1
   tbsp.
Well-beaten eggs, 2
Grated cheese (optional),
   4 tbsp.

Dissolve bouillon cubes in boiling water. Add potatoes, carrots, onions, tomatoes; season with salt and pepper. Add butter; cover. Simmer 15–20 minutes until vegetables are cooked. Taste and correct seasoning. Stir eggs slowly into broth; continue stirring another 3 minutes. Serve with grated cheese at the table. MAKES 3–4 SERVINGS.

Variation: Omit eggs, add 2 tbsp. rice or ½ cup broken vermicelli at same time as vegetables.

ROMAN CORN-MEAL SQUARES

*Nothing in the
house but*
   CANNED TOMATOES⁸, 1 No. 2 can
and
   CORN MEAL, ½ cup
and

Milk, 1¼ cups	Garlic clove, 1
Egg, 1	Chopped onion, ⅓ cup
Grated cheese, ¾ cup	Tomato paste (optional),
Salt, ¾ tsp.	half 3-ounce can
Pepper to taste	Salt and pepper to taste
Salad oil or melted butter,	Basil, ¼ tsp.
⅓ cup	

Substitute: 5 fresh—cut in slivers—plus 1 cup water or bouillon.

Gradually stir milk into corn meal. Cook very slowly, stirring constantly until mixture comes to a boil. Boil 5 minutes. Remove from heat; beat in egg. Add half the cheese, salt, and pepper. Stir in half the oil. Spread in 1½-inch-thick layer on floured board or baking sheet. Cool. Cut into squares. Place in shallow baking dish. Make a sauce by heating remaining oil in saucepan. Add garlic. Cook until brown. Remove garlic; add onion, tomatoes, and tomato paste. Season with salt, pepper, and basil. Simmer 10 minutes. Pour over corn meal. Top with remain-

ing cheese. Bake in medium hot 400° oven 30 minutes.
SERVES 3–4 AS A MAIN COURSE.

Variation: Add cooked green vegetable to sauce.

SALEM SPLIT PEA SOUP

*Nothing in the
house but*
    DRIED YELLOW SPLIT PEAS, 1 cup
and

Chopped onion, 3 tbsp.	Pepper to taste
Chopped carrot, 1 tbsp.	Ham or soup bones
Bouillon or stock, 1 quart	(optional)
Bay leaf, 1	Garlic toast, 4 slices
Salt, 1 tsp.	

Place split peas, onion, carrot, bouillon, bay leaf, salt,
pepper, and bones in soup pot. Bring to a boil. Lower
heat and simmer about 1 hour until peas are tender.
Serve with toast slices floating in soup. SERVES 4.

Variation: Sliced frankfurters or diced ham may be
added.

TOMATO PIE

*Nothing in the
house but*
    TOMATOES, 6 large, cut in ½-inch-thick slices
and
    PIECRUST MIX, ½ package
and

Salt and pepper to taste	Sugar, 1 tsp.
Corn meal[s], ½ cup	Grated cheese, ½ cup
Butter or margarine, 4	Melted butter, 1 tbsp.
tbsp.	

Substitute: Bread or cracker crumbs.

Prepare pie dough as directed on package for 1 crust.
Season tomatoes with salt and pepper. Coat with corn

meal. Fry in butter. Turn with spatula to brown both sides. Sprinkle each slice with pinch sugar. Line a piepan with pastry dough. Place a layer of tomatoes on the bottom. Sprinkle with grated cheese. Repeat a layer of tomatoes, then cheese. Continue until tomatoes are used up. Top with cheese. Sprinkle with melted butter. Bake in hot 425° oven 10 minutes. Lower heat, bake 15 minutes more. Serve piping hot. THIS CAN BE MAIN DISH FOR 2, OR SIDE DISH FOR 4.

Variation: Add slices of Swiss or Münster cheese and/or pot cheese to each layer.

Nothing in the House but Onions

FRENCH ONION SOUP

*Nothing in the
house but*
  ONIONS, sliced thin, 4–5 or more
and

Oil, olive or good salad oil, 3 tbsp.

Butter or margarine, 1 tbsp.

Flour, 1 tbsp.

Bouillon, cubes, canned, or concentrate, 6 cups

Salt and pepper to taste

Sugar, ½ tsp.

Toast, 4 slices, rubbed with garlic

Grated cheese, 4 tbsp.

Sauté onions in oil very slowly until soft. Add butter. When melted, sprinkle with flour. Stir until golden. Mix bouillon, salt, pepper, and sugar. Stir into onions. Simmer 10 minutes. Pour into 1 large or 4 individual small casseroles. Float toast on top. Sprinkle with cheese. Heat in moderate 375° oven 12 minutes. Serve piping hot. Sprinkle with more cheese at table. SERVES 4.

Suggested: This plus a vegetable salad makes a good meal—wonderful with ham sandwiches.

ONION PIE

*Nothing in the
house but*
  ONIONS, finely chopped, 2 cups
and

Hot roll mix, ½ package	Pitted black olives
Oil, 3 tbsp.	(optional), 12
Salt, ⅛ tsp.	Anchovy fillets (optional),
Pepper, ⅛ tsp.	cut in half lengthwise,
	about 6

Prepare dough as directed. Cover and let rise in warm
place until doubled in bulk. Meanwhile, cook onions, seasoned with salt and pepper, in oil over low heat for 20
minutes until puréed. Take care not to burn. Spread
dough on oiled baking dish. Brush with oil. Spread with
onion purée. Dot with pitted olives. Decorate with criss-
cross anchovy fillets. Bake in hot oven about 20 minutes.
Serve warm. SERVES 4.

ONION RAGOUT

*Nothing in the
house but*
  ONIONS, coarsely chopped, 1½ cups
and

Bacon, ham, or meat	Bouillon, ¼ cup
drippings, 3 tbsp.	Bay leaf, 1
Chopped green peppers, 2	Chopped parsley, ½ tsp.
Tomatoes (optional), 1½	Thyme, ¼ tsp.
cups	Salt and pepper to taste

Sauté onions with green peppers in drippings until soft.
Stir in tomatoes, bouillon, bay leaf, parsley, thyme, salt
and pepper. Bring slowly to a boil. Simmer very gently
about 15 minutes, stirring occasionally. Good sprinkled
with grated cheese. SERVES 2–3.

Variation No. 1: Drop in bread crumb balls and cook covered about 15 minutes.

Variation No. 2: Add peeled diced potatoes before adding tomatoes.

Nothing in the House but Potatoes

HOT BAKED POTATO SNACKS

*Nothing in the
house but*
  BAKING POTATOES, 4 large
and

Salad oil, about 3 tbsp.	Salt, 1½ tsp.
Bacon, 4–8 strips and/or bacon drippings	Pepper, ¼ tsp.
	Sugar, 2 tbsp.
Minced onion, ½ cup	Vinegar, ¼ cup plus 2 tbsp.
Minced green pepper or pimento, ¼ cup	

Rub potatoes with oil. Bake about 50 minutes or until done. Meanwhile, cook bacon until crisp. Remove and crumble. Measure drippings—if less than ⅔ cup, add salad oil. (If you lack bacon use meat drippings.) Cook onion, green pepper, salt, pepper, sugar, and vinegar in drippings, until onion is soft. When potatoes are done, cut thin slice from top. Scoop out insides, keeping shell intact. Mix with onion mixture and stuff back in shells. MAKES 4 SERVINGS.

Variation: Add 2–3 tbsp. of any finely chopped leftover meat, fish, fowl, hard-boiled egg, cooked spinach, cheese, etc.

POTATO CAKE TURNOVER

Nothing in the
house but
  POTATOES, 4 medium
and

Butter or margarine, 2 tbsp.	Salt and pepper to taste
Flour, ¼ cup	Eggs, 2
Milk, ½–¾ cup	Grated cheese, 2 tbsp.
	Olive oil, 2 tbsp.

Boil potatoes until tender. Peel and put through ricer. Melt 1 tbsp. butter; blend in flour. Add milk gradually, stirring constantly until thick and smooth. Add potatoes and remaining butter, salt, and pepper. If mixture seems too dry, add a little milk. Cool slightly; beat in eggs and grated cheese. Heat olive oil in frying pan, making sure to cover bottom and sides. Add potato mixture. Cook about 15–20 minutes over medium heat, shaking pan occasionally to prevent sticking. When crisp and brown, invert onto a platter. SERVES 4.

PIEDMONT GNOCCHI, PRONOUNCED KNEE-OH'-KEY

Nothing in the
house but
  POTATOES, boiled and peeled, 10–12
and

Butter or margarine, 4 tbsp.	Grated cheese, ½ cup
Beaten eggs (optional), 1–2	Boiling water, 5 quarts seasoned with 3 tbsp. salt
Salt, ½ tbsp.	Butter, 1 tbsp.
Pepper, ½ tsp.	Mushroom or tomato sauce
Nutmeg, ¼ tsp.	
Flour, 1¼ cups	

Mash potatoes with butter. Add eggs, salt, pepper, nutmeg. Work flour into potatoes, kneading thoroughly. Add

more flour if necessary. Cut "dough" into 4-inch pieces.
Roll into long ropes ½ inch thick. Cut into 1-inch lengths.
Cook no more than 15 at a time. Boil about 6 minutes.
Gnocchi will rise to surface. Remove with strainer, or
slotted spoon. Keep water boiling. Repeat until all the
gnocchi are cooked. Arrange in layers in baking dish.
Sprinkle each layer with grated cheese. Top with dots
of butter. Pop under broiler to brown. Many eat this piled
high like spaghetti, covered with a thick mushroom or
tomato sauce. THIS CAN BE MAIN DISH FOR 2. OR A SIDE DISH
FOR 4.

POTATO BLINTZES

*Nothing in the
house but*
POTATOES, 4–5 medium
and

Beaten egg yolk, 1	Milk[s], 1½ cups
Salt, ¼ tsp.	Flour, 1 cup
Sugar, ¼ tsp.	Stiffly beaten egg white, 1
Melted butter or	
margarine, ½ tsp.	

FILLING:

Chopped onion, ½ cup	Bouillon or potato water,
Meat drippings, fat, or oil,	5 tbsp.
3 tbsp.	Salt, ⅛ tsp.
	Pepper, ¼ tsp.

Substitute: ¾ cup milk and ¾ cup water.

Boil potatoes until tender. Meanwhile, beat egg yolk with
salt, sugar, butter, and milk. Add flour; stir briskly until
batter is smooth. Fold in egg white. Butter 6-inch skillet
very lightly. Pour in a very thin layer of batter—just
enough to cover bottom of pan. Cook on one side only
until golden brown. Turn onto wax paper. Repeat until
batter is used up.
Prepare filling: Peel potatoes. Sauté onion in drippings.

Mix in potatoes, mashing them in frying pan. Moisten with bouillon. Season with salt and pepper. Spoon a heaping tbsp. of filling onto the fried side of each blintz. Fold two sides into filling, fold one end over other. Fry in butter until brown. SERVES 4 AS A MAIN DISH.

POTATO LATKES

Nothing in the
house but
    POTATOES, 8 large, peeled and grated
and
    EGGS, 1 or 2 separated
and

Flour, 1 tbsp.	Butter or shortening, 3–5
Grated onion (optional),	tbsp.
1 small	Applesauce or sour cream
Salt and pepper to taste	

Mix grated, then well-drained potatoes with egg yolks, flour, onion, salt, and pepper. Fold in stiffly beaten egg whites. Heat butter or shortening in frying pan. Drop in potato mixture from a spoon. Flatten. Fry until golden brown on both sides. Drain on absorbent paper. Serve hot with either applesauce or sour cream, sugared or not as preferred. SERVES 4.

Suggested: Add bacon and coffee and you have a wonderful lunch or late supper menu. We say 8 large potatoes—but even 10 would not be too many.

POTATOES GRATIN

Nothing in the
house but
   POTATOES, 8 large, peeled and sliced crossways
and
   GRATED SWISS CHEESE, ¼ pound
and

Beaten egg, 1	Nutmeg, dash
Milk[8], 1½ cups	Garlic, 1 clove
Salt and pepper to taste	Butter, 2 tbsp.

   Substitute: Evaporated milk and water, or chicken soup, or cube and boiling water.

Mix egg with milk, salt, pepper, nutmeg, and sliced potatoes. Add half the cheese. Mix well. Pour into buttered baking dish that has first been rubbed with cut garlic. Dot with butter. Top with remaining cheese. Bake in moderate 350° oven for 1 hour. SERVES 4.

INDEX